MW00513198

INSIDE OUT

STRENGTHENING THE CORE OF YOUR FAITH

MIKE HOLT

Unless otherwise noted, all Scriptures are taken from The Holy Bible: New International Version. Grand Rapids: Zondervan, 1984, 2011

How To Use This Resource—The breakdown of this spiritual workout

As you will see from the table of contents, this book contains 18 chapters broken down into 6 different sections. This provides the opportunity to complete Inside Out over the course of 18 weeks or 6 weeks, whichever works best for your needs.

The 18 Week Journey—Complete as an individual, small group, or one-on-one journey!

- Individual journey— Read one chapter per week. Each week, there is a teaching video that expands on the material covered in the chapter. You can purchase access to the discipleship videos on the book's website www.ministryresourcehub.com/insideout. Once you purchase access to the videos, you will be able to download fill-in-the-blank guides that follow the teaching.

- Small Group Journey—The flow of Inside Out is conducive to doing three different rounds of small groups. Look quickly at the table of contents. You would do this the following way:

    - Small group series #1: 6 weeks covering sections one & two

    - Small group series #2: 6 weeks covering sections three & four

    - Small group series #3: 6 weeks covering sections five & six

    Note: Small groups desiring to do the 18-week journey would use the same videos as the individual journey.

- One-on-one Journey—This is, in my opinion, the best way to walk through any discipleship resource. Preferably, seasoned believers would mentor younger believers or brand new Christians. In a perfect world, the discipler and the student would watch the videos together or on their own and meet to discuss the content each week. Churches could also launch discipleship based small groups composed of a few pairs of mentors and students. However you decide to engage in the one-on-one journey, there are additional tools available on the website to facilitate the discipleship process.

The 6-week Journey–Complete as an individual, small group, or one-on-one journey!

The videos for the six-week journey to be used by an individual or small group can also be accessed by purchasing the "Six Week Journey" on the website. The six-week journey is more of a discipleship crash course, if you will. Downloadable fill-in-the-blank guides, small group questions, and talking points for mentors are available as well. You will finish the book in six weeks by reading the following content in the book and watching the available videos online:

Week 1–Chapters 1-3

Week 2–Chapters 4-6

Week 3–Chapters 7-9

Week 4–Chapters 10-12

Week 5–Chapters 13-15

Week 6–Chapters 16-18

However you decide to embrace Inside Out, my prayer is that you are strengthened in your faith and inspired to fulfill the Great Commission. We are called to follow Jesus closely and to make disciples as we do. That is the heart behind this resource!

CONTENTS

SECTION 1

CHAPTER 1

Understanding the spiritual C.O.R.E.

Congratulations on your decision to grow spiritually! Whether you are a new believer, a Christian looking for a fresh start in your faith, or a mature Christ follower desiring to learn how to disciple others, this book will provide a new beginning for you in your walk with God. The decision to intentionally grow in your relationship with Christ and the decision to help others do the same are two of the most important decisions you can make as a Christian. This book will empower you to do just that from the inside out. Look at the verse that inspired this book and take note of the words I have italicized for you. From this point forward, we will refer to this verse as the CORE verse of this book.

Philippians 2:12-13 Therefore, my dear friends, as you have always obeyed—not only in my presence, but now much more in my absence—continue to *work out* your salvation with fear and trembling, for it is God who works *in* you to will and to act in order to fulfill his good purpose. (Italics added).

This is one of my favorite verses in the Bible because it clearly communicates the vital truth that spiritual growth is an inside-out process. We are called to work out what God is working within us through the help of the Holy Spirit. And this work out begins with strengthening our spiritual CORE.

Working Out Your Core

I grew up playing competitive soccer. However, I was born with zero arches in my feet. These two things were not a good combination. Playing with flat feet resulted in terrible shin splints on the field. As I got older, the pain started traveling from my feet, up my legs, and into my lower back. The wear and tear on my body eventually contributed to the degeneration of a couple of discs in my back. I would half-heartedly attempt to address these issues from time to time, but eventually I ended up with a back surgery later on in life.

Facing the possibility of a second, more invasive surgery, the doctor said something that the Holy Spirit would use to burn a thought into my soul about my spiritual life. He was looking at an MRI of my spine and said, "If you weren't sitting here with me and I didn't know you were in your 30's, I would guess by looking at your MRI that you were 60 years old." Ouch! Not what I wanted to hear. I asked him if I could do anything at all to prevent the second surgery. He simply said, "You will have to attack and strengthen your core."

He then went on to explain the CORE muscles in our body such as our stomach and lower back muscles provide the foundation for the rest of our overall skeletal health and strength. Along with improved eating he explained that strengthening my core would be the starting point for overhauling my physical body. The more I pondered this dialogue, the more I realized how true this is for our spiritual health as well.

As Christians we have a spiritual CORE. This CORE consists of four disciplines that serve as the backbone of our Christianity. Much like the muscles that comprise the physical core of our body, these four disciplines are connected to each other and are vital to our walk with God. They also must be exercised for us to be spiritually strong. The four CORE disciplines of the Christian life are:

C-Connect With God

O-Offer God Your Everything

R-Release Your Ministry

E-Engage in Personal Outreach and Missions

We were created for these four things but when they are not being exercised our overall spiritual health can be compromised. Again, I think back to the issues with my back. The issues I have had with my spine are connected to my flat feet. Because the foundation was flat, a whole host of problems manifested in my body.

The same is true spiritually. If any of these four dynamics are flat in your spiritual life, they can cause the rest of your walk with God to be out of alignment and potentially lead to other issues for you as well. But if these core muscles are strong, they provide the Holy Spirit the ground-work needed to help grow you into the man or woman of God you are created to be.

Not willpower but will empowered!

However, before you begin this journey, let me emphasize again the first 8 words of Philippians 2:13, "for it is God who works *in you* to will and to act in order to fulfill his good purpose." (Italics added.)

It is God working in you to empower you to live out your faith. I take great encouragement in this truth! I am not alone in this spiritual work out. God is with me and His Holy Spirit is in me, empowering me from within to work out my faith successfully. As you will learn in chapter 3,

> *It isn't about will power; it is about our will*
> *<u>empowered</u> by the Holy Spirit.*

The Holy Spirit infuses us with power to press on to maturity. That is the purpose of the Bible reading and prayer plan that I have included throughout the book. Tapping into the power provided by the Holy Spirit is necessary if we are going to work out what God is working in us.

I am grateful for your desire to allow God to grow you from the inside out! My prayer is that you will enjoy the journey while also being challenged to grow in an intentional way through this resource. I pray that you will grasp the four CORE disciplines of the Christian faith as God's design to grow you as a disciple. And I pray that you will capture a heart to mentor other believers to do the same.

Weekly Spiritual Workout and Questions

At the conclusion of every chapter you will notice a weekly spiritual workout that is provided for you. This weekly workout will include Bible reading and other exercises to help cultivate spiritual growth in your life. The questions provided at the end of each week are there to foster personal reflection as well as discussion starters between you and your mentor or with your small group.

Week 1 Spiritual Workout:

- Let's start working out together by turning to appendix #1 and filling out the CORE evaluation sheet. It will provide you with insight into the health of your own spiritual CORE and provide you with some valuable talking points between you and your mentor or small group.

- Read the next chapter in this book.

Reflection Questions For Individual or Small Group Use

1. When it comes to starting a spiritual workout such as the one this book provides, what is your biggest fear or hesitation with this kind of commitment? What makes you the most excited?

2. In this chapter, Mike compared our physical core to our spiritual core. What are some other ways we can compare a physical workout to a spiritual workout? How are they similar and how are they different?

3. What are some of the benefits to working out both physically and spiritually? What makes it so hard to stay committed to both kinds of workouts?

CHAPTER 2

Inside Out Salvation

The Greatest Story Ever Told

Everyone loves a good story. I personally love action movies. Air Force One & The Fugitive are two of my favorites. I can still hear Harrison Ford declaring to the traitor who betrayed him to the Russians, "Get off my plane!" Ahh....love that moment. And how about my absolute favorite movie of all time, Rocky 4? My adrenaline starts pumping just thinking about Rocky's epic training scene. Whether you are into action movies, comedies, or even those Hallmark movies my wife loves to watch—every one of us loves a good story. We watch them. We read them. We binge on them. We love a good story!

There are fundamental ingredients to every good story. For example, every good story has a hero and a villain. Every good story involves a crisis to be solved or a battle to be fought. And every good story, including ones that leave us talking about them long after the closing credits are the ones that have plot twists, interesting characters, and even cliff hangers. You take these elements out of a story and it is very, very boring. The movie is turned off halfway through. The book is put down and never finished. And the Netflix series doesn't make it to the next episode.

But the truth is, the greatest story ever told is called the gospel—which simply means "good news." And boy, does it have every element imaginable of a good storyline.

- There is a villain in this story named Satan.

- There is a hero named Jesus.

- There are main characters—you, me, and especially God.

- And there is a huge crisis that must be resolved called the fall of man.

And interlaced within the story of Jesus are plot twists and surprise storylines. Just think about Jesus shocking the devil and shaking the demonic forces of hell to their very core with His resurrection from the dead. There is also the cliffhanger called the second coming of Christ. Since the time Jesus ascended back into heaven the church of Jesus Christ has been on the edge of its seat, anxiously waiting for Him to come back and get his people once and for all. What a story.

But unlike a movie or a Hulu original series, this story is absolutely one hundred percent true. None of it is fabricated or fictional. It hasn't been shortened to fit our time frame and the picture has not been adjusted to fit a certain screen size. Jesus Christ came to this earth, died on a cross, was raised to life three days later, and went back into heaven so that one day you and I could be with Him there. It doesn't get any better, or any truer, than that. It's the greatest story ever told, and the final chapters are still unfolding before us. And it is a story we are invited to live and experience personally through our faith in Jesus Christ.

This chapter breaks down this true story of the good news called "salvation." My prayer is that you understand it again through fresh eyes of faith. Let's recommit to continue in our salvation and embrace the greatest story ever told again—from the inside out!

The Reason For Our Salvation

There are a few movies I can watch over and over again. One of them is Castaway. My wife rolls her eyes every time I stop to watch some of it when I come across it on one of those obscure channels on TV. (She can roll her eyes all she wants. I'm the one who has to endure the Hallmark movies.)

In the movie, Tom Hanks plays a FedEx airline pilot whose plane crashes and he finds himself lost on a deserted island. He has no clue where his plane has gone down and he's all alone. In fact, he's so alone he eventually becomes best friends with a volleyball he affectionately names Wilson. Can you still hear him shouting "Wilson!" "Wilson!" during his final attempt to get off the island? That's classic film writing if you ask me.

Most of the movie is about Tom Hanks trying to survive while enduring the terrible and immense loneliness he experiences during almost a decade of being lost as a Castaway. Finally, after years of studying the weather patterns of the island and making a raft big enough to survive the massive waves that would come against him, he was finally saved. He was finally found. Wilson wasn't so lucky.

Can we flip channels for a minute to another story about being lost and found? It's the story of our spiritual state before God apart from Christ. This story actually started in the Garden of Eden thousands of years ago. God created Adam and Eve and placed them in this special garden for one reason– to have a close and personal relationship with them and eventually all of creation, including you and me. Imagine that. God, whose vast character is described in the Bible with such descriptors as all powerful, all knowing, and supreme over all the earth has chosen to share Himself with mankind. This is simply remarkable.

But something tragic happens. Adam and Eve chose to sin which meant physical and spiritual death entered into humanity's script. Romans 3:23 says, "For *all* have sinned and fallen short of the glory of God." (Italics added). All. That includes you and me. But it gets worse. Romans 6:23 then says, "For the wages of sin is death." What you and I deserve for sinning against a Holy God who has never sinned is the spiritual punishment of eternal separation from Him in a place called hell.

We are all guilty–plain and simple. And if it wasn't for Christ, our story would end miserably. But unlike a movie with a terrible ending, there is good news in this story of the gospel. There is a pivotal plot twist about to take place.

The Remedy To Sin

Beyond the garden of Eden, the rest of the Old Testament can briefly be summarized as man continuously in rebellion against God and/or trying to gain good standing with Him again through the law and good works. Again, these efforts would prove dismally unsuccessful, but God would eventually turn the page and start a new chapter in human history called the New Testament. While the Old Testament begins with man dying spiritually as a result of sin, the New Testament begins with Jesus, the one who came to give us spiritual life again. He came to rescue us, redeem us, and ultimately to restore us back to the Father. It reminds me of another one of my favorite movies–The Guardian.

Kevin Costner plays Ben Randall, an elite rescue swimmer in the United States Coastguard. After tragically losing his crew in an accident, he is sent to teach at the most prestigious training school for future rescue swimmers. There he meets Jake Fischer, played by Ashton Kutcher, who is a rising star within his class but is also young, arrogant, and comes with his own set of baggage. During this unfolding story, Jake sets out to break every one of Ben's swimming records, but he is told there is one record that he would never break. Apparently, his new mentor had once held on to a rescued man high above the raging ocean from his helicopter with one hand and refused to let go–ripping tendons in his arm as a result.

After graduation, Ben and Jake go on a rescue mission together, risking their lives, and finding themselves in a heart harrowing scene. The young Jake finds himself holding on to Ben, his mentor, in the exact same fashion that Ben had done with someone else all those years ago. Jake, recalling the story told to him about Ben's bravery, looks at him and says, "I'll never let go." And he was sincere. He would have hung on through the pain of tendons tearing in his arm as well. But to do so in this case would jeopardize the helicopter and the entire crew. And so, Ben, understanding the danger this posed to Jake and his team, unwrapped his glove and chose to drop to his death in the ocean below. He willingly gave up his life so the crew could live. That is what a hero does. And that is what Jesus did for you and me.

Romans 6:23 says, "the wages of sin is death, but the gift of God is eternal life in Christ Jesus our Lord." Sin, in its simplest definition, means missing the mark of God's standard for heaven. It is disobedience against God that brings with it the ultimate penalty—spiritual death which means remaining separated from Him forever. However, because God is love, He sent His one and only son to die in our place. In fact, Jesus said of himself in Luke 19:10, "the son of man came to seek and save that which was lost." Jesus came as a heavenly guardian on a massive search and rescue mission and took the punishment for our sin upon his back so we would not perish. In other words, he unstrapped the glove from his hand. No, actually, he took nails driven into his hands, and willingly laid down his life for us on a wooden cross. And the result was that you and I could receive the gift of salvation as a free gift, though it cost Jesus his very life. Everyone needs to exercise their right to this gift purchased by the blood of Jesus!

The Right Of Our Salvation

John 1:12 says, "Yet to all who did receive him, to those who believed in his name, he gave the right to become children of God." Because of what Jesus did, we have the right to now become children of God who have entered into an eternal relationship with Him as our heavenly Father. But how? It's really simple—by faith. Ephesians 2:8-9 says, "For it is by grace you have been saved, through faith, and this is not from yourselves, it is the gift of God, not by works, so that no one can boast." It is by faith we are saved. That's it. We trust and believe in what Jesus Christ has already done to secure our salvation and invite Him to be Lord of our life. Romans 10:9 tells us how this expression of faith happens, "If you declare with your mouth, 'Jesus is Lord,' and believe in your heart that God raised him from the dead, you will be saved." Simply place your faith in what He has already done and invite Him to be the Lord of your life. Do so and your sins will be forgiven, you will receive heaven as a free gift, and you will start an eternal relationship with God who desires to interact with you on a daily basis. The rest of this book is essentially about deepening this intimacy with God as the Holy Spirit empowers you from the inside out!

Note to mature Christians

I realize that comparing our great salvation to movies may seem a bit underwhelming. Keep in mind that this chapter is geared toward those who have just become a Christian and that you may be mentoring now using this material. This first chapter sets up the rest of the book which dives into deeper waters. Also keep in mind that the videos on the book's website provides deeper content for anyone who wants a little more meat!

Week 2 Spiritual Workout

- Read through the content in the shaded fresh start box. Prayerfully ask the Lord if you should be baptized in this season of your life. As you read through it, you'll see that I personally have no issue with someone being baptized for a second time. If you have just given your life to Christ or rededicated yourself to the Lord, I believe being baptized is something you should absolutely do. It is actually a command and an act of obedience.

- The second aspect to this week's workout is making sure you have a good Bible to read. Bible reading will be an integral part of the weekly workouts from this point forward. Sometimes buying a new Bible in a renewed spiritual season is impactful. I personally use the NIV version.

- Recommit yourself to being faithful in church attendance. Remember, you need others around you to grow, and that is what the local church is for! My challenge to you is to not miss one Sunday in church as you are working through this resource.

- Read the next chapter in this book.

Reflection Questions For Individual or Small Group Use

1. Can you think of any other movies that might be a good portrayal of the gospel?

2. Do you really grasp that salvation is by faith and not by works? In other words, we can never earn our way to heaven. Jesus had to pay for it, and we must receive it by faith. Is this a spiritual concept you truly understand? How does the understanding that salvation is by faith and not works change someone's approach to their spiritual life?

3. Scripture is clear, "the wages of sin is death." (Romans 6:23) Jesus paid the ultimate price for our sin by dying on the cross. Those who believe in Him are saved, become children of God, and receive heaven as a free gift. Those who do not remain separated from Him and will spend eternity in hell. How does the concept of hell resonate with you? Does it seem "fair" that God would allow someone to go to hell? Why or why not?

CHAPTER 3

Inside Out Holy Spirit

My marriage proposal to Carla seems like only yesterday. If you are married, I'm not sure how your marriage proposal went down, but this is my story.....

First, I took Carla to Applebee's. (Don't judge. I was young and broke.) There at Applebee's I shared my calling and life dream with her once again. We talked deeply of the dreams we had for the future. Afterwards, I took her on a journey.

I wanted to revisit all of the places that meant something special to us while we were dating. For example, we met our first year in college at an ice cream social that a college ministry was hosting for new freshmen in a building called The Tate Center at the University of Georgia. (Go Bulldogs!) We went there first and laughed about the first time we met. We then visited the fountain where we used to sit and talk on north campus. And from there, we went to our favorite dining hall and even our favorite bus stop. Every place we stopped was significant and special to our story in some way.

Our last stop was at the church where I was a youth pastor. It was like 2am in the morning by the time we arrived. Lucky for me, the 12 red roses I spread out over the altar had not died. The slow romantic playlist I set up was still looping in the background.

I knew I was called to be a preacher, so I sat her down in a nice chair right in front of the altar and proceeded to speak a message about my love for her.

I think at this point she knew what I was up to. The tears were welling up in her eyes. At the conclusion of my "sermon" I recapped our history and spoke about my hopes for an amazing future together. I took a knee, pulled out the ring, and popped the question.

Thankfully for me, she said YES!

And the rest is history.

This is my proposal story. This is what I did to woo my wife to myself and to bring our story to a point where I kneeled before her and said, "Only you baby. Only you!"

Let's get spiritual for a minute

You say, "how in the world does your proposal story have anything to do with this book especially when this chapter is all about the Holy Spirit!" Thank you for asking.

When Carla and I were dating, and long before I proposed, I did several other things to woo her and draw her to myself. From the small fake rose I bought her at a gas station one time to make her laugh, to the many walks we took on campus, to the meals I paid for when we went out on our dates—all of these are instances of how I drew her to myself.

And God does the exact same thing with us at salvation. He draws us to Himself by the Holy Spirit! He woos us away from other "gods", including the god of self and sin, and brings us to a point where we kneel our hearts to him and say, "Only You God! Only You!"

But we need to pause here and take a short road trip together. (Something else Carla and I did from time to time.) Let's make sure we are all clear on who I am talking about when I say, "the Holy Spirit."

The Holy Spirit is the third person of the Trinity. The term "Trinity" is the theological word describing what Christianity teaches about the nature of God. We believe that He is a triune God—meaning He consists of three distinct and divine persons in one. These three are God the Father, God the Son (Jesus), and God the Holy Spirit. Each person of the Trinity also has a distinct personality with character traits that reveal the totality of the God we serve and express the breadth of His love for us. If you read Matthew 3:13-17, you will see each person of the Trinity at work. God is three in one and each person of the trinity has deeply intertwined yet distinct roles in our lives. And when it comes to the Holy Spirit, His role actually starts in our lives before our point of salvation.

The Holy Spirit Who Draws Us
Jesus said in John 6:44 "No one can come to me unless the Father who sent me draws him." He also said in John 12:32, "But I, when I am lifted up from the earth, will draw all men to myself." Jesus is saying in these two passages that once he is crucified (lifted up from the earth) and resurrected, the Holy Spirit of God will be active in the world, wooing and drawing people to a full understanding of their need for a Savior. 2 Peter 3:9 says, "God is patient, not wanting anyone to perish but for all to come to repentance." And so, the Spirit of God is at work in the world, drawing people to the Father. He will use the good, the bad, and the ugly parts of your history to bring forth *his story* in your life.

That is certainly what took place with me. I did not grow up in a Christian home. In high school, I started hanging around these Christian kids on my campus and hearing phrases such as "born again" but had no idea what they meant. At the same time, I started dating a girl who came to me one day and told me she had been raped. I did everything I could to help her but was obviously limited as a seventeen-year-old boy. However, she swore me to secrecy and eventually I became quite helpless with the entire situation.

Finally, the situation became too much for me to handle and I sought out the leader of this Christian ministry, trying to find someone that I could confide in. Her name was Dee Dee. She graciously invited me to her home where we talked about this situation for several hours; thinking through the best way to get my girlfriend the help she so desperately needed. On the way out of her house, Dee Dee asked me if there was anything else I needed to talk about. I nonchalantly said, "Yeah. What does it mean to be saved? I've been hearing that term a lot lately."

And that's all that it took. She sat me back down, shared the gospel with me, and I became overwhelmed with a sense of God's presence in that room. I simply said, "I need that!" And, weeping into my Spud McKenzie shirt (yes, the mascot of Budweiser during that time) I gave my life to Christ. And the rest is history. Or should I say, the rest is *His story.*

Not long after my girlfriend called me crying, having no idea I had just gotten saved. She needed me to come over. I walked into her kitchen and she said, "I have to tell you something." I thought she was battling depression again from the sexual assault. But instead she said, "Everything I've been telling you for the last year is a complete lie!" I was dumbfounded. But then I remembered something that Dee Dee shared with me. She said, "Before you go, let me share one verse with you. Romans 8:28 says, 'And we know that in all things God works for the good of those who love him, who have been called according to his purpose.'" Suddenly, standing there in the kitchen looking my girlfriend in the eyes, I understood the word "all" in that verse! The truth is, if my girlfriend had never lied to me, I would have never sat in Dee Dee's house that night and received Christ. God had used all things to lead me to Himself. In my case, He used someone else's lie to lead me to the truth. And He did so through the Holy Spirit that was already working in my heart as I got involved in a Christian based ministry before even getting saved. To avoid trying to sound like I am throwing this girlfriend under the bus, the truth is she is the one who encouraged me to get involved in this Christian based ministry in the first place and it was through her and her family that I became spiritually rooted after getting saved. Let me say it again, all things. All. God truly is not willing for anyone to perish and He uses the Holy Spirit to draw people to Himself. He can use anything and anyone to do so.

The Holy Spirit Who Is a Deposit

One spiritual principle that is foundational to your entire Christian faith is that at the point of your salvation, the Holy Spirit takes up residency in your life. Your physical body, in fact, becomes his very temple and your heart becomes His home. One central verse in the Bible we must all know is Romans 8:11,

"And if the Spirit of him who raised Jesus from the dead is living in you, he who raised Christ from the dead will also give life to your mortal bodies because of his Spirit who lives in you."

The same spirit that raised Christ from the dead now lives in you and me as well. Let that sink in for a moment. The same powerful spirit that God exerted in Christ when He raised his own son from death is now the very power source that lives in us (Ephesians 1:20)!

The Bible also tells us that it is by this Spirit that we are born again and able to call God Almighty our heavenly "Father" (Romans 8:15). And to top it all off, this Holy Spirit is also called a deposit, guaranteeing something that is even better to come (Ephesians 1:14). In other words, as powerful and amazing as the Holy Spirit within us is right now, it is also a down-payment on an inheritance of something even greater to come—heaven itself.

Wow, now you can see why I said what I said in the introduction to this book:

Christianity is not about will power. It is about our will empowered by God Himself, through the Person of the Holy Spirit, from the inside out.

The Holy Spirit Who Develops Us

Now that the Holy Spirit has drawn us to the Father and now that He lives inside of us, He is continuously at work developing us into the kind of Christian God has created us to be. Look one more time at Philippians 2:12-13 and notice the italics I have added.

"Therefore, my dear friends, as you have always obeyed—not only in my presence, but now much more in my absence—continue to work out your salvation with fear and trembling, *for it is God who works in you to will and to act according to His good pleasure.*"

For it is God who works in you.

Wow! God is both with us and He is working in us by the Holy Spirit. He works within us for two primary reasons. The first is to instill an awareness of God's presence into our lives. By cultivating intimacy with God through the Holy Spirit, we grow beyond head knowledge to heart knowledge of the Lord. (Ephesians 1:17) This is how our Christian walk excels to new levels. There is nothing like sensing the presence and nearness of God in our lives. Nothing. And this is possible by the Holy Spirit.

Secondly, the Holy Spirit is at work in our lives to make us more like Jesus. The very word "Christian" means "little Christ ones" and that is what the Holy Spirit's ultimate goal is in our lives–helping us to become more like the one whose name we bear. 2 Corinthians 3:18 says, "And we all, who with unveiled faces contemplate the Lord's glory, are being transformed into his image with ever-increasing glory, which comes from the Lord, who is the Spirit."

The Spirit within us desires to develop us from the inside out, transforming us from one level of Christlikeness to another. In fact, there are nine aspects of Christlikeness known as the fruit of the Holy Spirit found in Galatians 5:22-23, "But the fruit of the Spirit is love, joy, peace, patience, kindness, goodness, faithfulness, gentleness and self-control." The Spirit of God, as we remain in Christ and His Word remains in us, produces and develops these qualities in and through our character. Sometimes this work feels fun and amazing and sometimes it feels like surgery to our soul. But ultimately, everything the Holy Spirit does within us is for our good and for the Father's glory.

Special Note

By now, you can probably tell that I like alliteration-ha! Let me give you one more word that starts with the letter "D." That word is "dynamis." This is the Greek word for the word "power" in Acts 1:8, "But you will receive *power* when the Holy Spirit comes on you; and you will be my witnesses in Jerusalem, and in all Judea and Samaria, and to the ends of the earth." (italics included)

One role of the Holy Spirit is to empower the church to be witnesses of Jesus all across this world. Some believers view this work of the Holy Spirit as a second and distinct work known as the baptism of the Holy Spirit.

I expand on this subject in another appendix that can be downloaded on the book's website. Regardless of your viewpoint in how the Holy Spirit empowers the believer, we can all agree that Scripture is clear that the Holy Spirit does in fact empower the believer to fulfill their role in the Great Commission.

Week 3 Spiritual Workout

- Write out the story of how you became a Christian. This story is called your "testimony." Your testimony is your firsthand account of what Jesus has done in your life. Appendix 2 in the back of the book will guide you through this. It may just be the most important three paragraphs you will ever write!

- Read the next chapter in this book.

Individual and Small Group Reflection Questions:

1. What is your salvation story? Looking back on it, what people, places, and things did God use to bring you to Himself?

2. Romans 8:28 says, "For we know in all things, God works together for the good of those who love him." What are some circumstances or events of your life that God used to draw you to the point of salvation? What are some things from your past that He has worked together for your good? What are some of the things in your life now that you are trusting God to also work for your good?

3. Read Galatians 5:22-23 again. Which aspects of the fruit of the Holy Spirit do you feel strong in? Weak? Which one would you like to grow in as a result of reading through this book and drawing closer to God?

SECTION 2
CONNECTING WITH GOD

Welcome to section 2 of our spiritual workout! This is where we start the nitty gritty practical side of building our spiritual muscles. Remember, there are four different muscle groups we are looking to build that comprise the CORE of our faith:

C-Connect with God

O-Offer God Everything

R-Release Your Ministry

E-Engage In Personal Outreach and Missions

In this second section, consisting of three chapters, we will discuss an incredible privilege we have as believers-connecting personally with the Almighty, all-knowing, all-loving God of the universe. Just imagine that. The creator of the world who spun the stars and galaxies into place desires to spend time with you. In fact, He passionately longs for you and yearns to reveal more of Himself to you in an intimate and meaningful way. The God of the Bible is an experiential God who has provided three primary ways to connect with Him that we will explore in the following chapters:

Chapter 3: Inside-Out Bible, Connecting With God through His Word

Chapter 4: Inside-Out Prayer, Connecting With God Through Prayer

Chapter 5: Inside-Out Church, Connecting With God Through Fellowship With His People

Grab a pen and get ready to highlight, underline, and circle the deep truths and practical insights in the next three chapters!

"Therefore, my dear friends, as you have always obeyed—not only in my presence, but now much more in my absence—continue to work out your salvation with fear and trembling, for it is God who works in you to will and to act according to his good purpose." Philippians 2:12-13

Let's continue to work out by discovering how to connect with the God of the universe!

CHAPTER 4

Inside Out Bible Reading

Building Your Life Upon the Rock

This chapter begins exploring the first of the four C.O.R.E disciplines of the Christian faith outlined in this book: Connecting with God. The very first way we connect with Him is through His Word—known as the Bible. The word Bible comes from the Greek word biblios which means collection of books or booklets. A book in the Bible is a collection of writing devoted to a particular subject. The Bible is a collection of 66 books and letters divided into the Old and New Testament. Here are the major differences between the two testaments:

- The Old Testament contains 39 books and the New Testament contains 27 books.

- The Old Testament was originally written in the Hebrew language and the New Testament was originally written in the Greek language. Parts of the New Testament were also written in Aramaic.

- The Old Testament is about the history of mankind and God's dealing with man before Christ. The New Testament is God's dealing with man from the birth of Christ and beyond.

- The Old Testament is the story of the Israelites—a nation of people God selected to represent the type of relationship He desired with the entire world. The New Testament is the story of how Christ made this relationship available to everyone.

- The Old Testament is primarily about man's effort to secure salvation for himself through the law and by offering a multitude of blood sacrifices. (This was called The Old Covenant). The New Testament is about God's effort to come to us and to secure salvation for us by the death and resurrection of His Son, Jesus (known as The New Covenant).

Both Testaments are necessary to understanding the nature of God and both Testaments are actually about Jesus Christ when you get right down to it. In fact, a saying I heard when I first became a Christian was, "In the Old Testament Jesus is *concealed*, in the New Testament He is *revealed*." And that is ultimately the case. As you read the Old Testament, you read several stories and illustrations that represent Christ in the New Testament. These are called Biblical types. And when you read the New Testament you see the fullness of God's love manifested by the life, death, and resurrection of Jesus. You should also know that the Bible was written over a span of 1500 years, on 3 different continents, by over 40 different authors. Yet when you put the whole Bible together you discover one overarching theme—the salvation of mankind through Jesus Christ! The Bible is from the mouth of God, spoken by the breath of the One who is timeless, eternally true, and absolutely trustworthy and perfect in all His ways toward us.

The Bible is Inspired, Infallible, and Inerrant
2 Timothy 3:16 says, "All Scripture is God-breathed and is useful for teaching, rebuking, correcting and training in righteousness, so that the servant of God may be thoroughly equipped for every good work."

"All Scripture is God-breathed". These five words are fundamental to our Christian faith and what we believe about the Bible.

- These five words reveal that the Bible is ***inspired***-meaning that God himself wrote His book through men by divinely prompting and directing men's thoughts as they wrote the Bible. Because all Scripture is God breathed, all of it is useful to our daily lives. From the very front of the Bible to the very back, God wants to speak to us through His Word and use His Word to shape every facet of our lives.

- Because it is inspired, it is also ***infallible.*** Infallible means that God's word is absolutely true and therefore trustworthy. Psalms 33:4 says, "For the word of the LORD is right and true; he is faithful in all he does." His Word is right and true and absolutely trustworthy from generation to generation.

- Not only is it inspired and infallible, but it is also ***inerrant.*** Inerrant simply means that God's Word is perfect and without error because He Himself is perfect. Psalm 18:30 says, "As for God, his way is perfect: The LORD's word is flawless; he shields all who take refuge in him." In a flawed world full deception that leaves the soul empty, God and His word are a refuge to run to and find true rest.

God's written Word is indeed inspired, infallible, and inerrant but it is still more than a collection of God's thoughts on paper. The Bible is God Himself revealed through Jesus, The Living Word.

Jesus: The Living Word Whose Words Are "Spirit & Life"

Speaking of Jesus, John 1:1-2 says, "In the beginning was the Word, and the Word was with God, and the Word was God." John presents Jesus as the personal Word of God to mankind. Just as a person's words reveal his true character, Jesus as "the Living Word" reveals the heart and mind of God to you and me. John continues, "the Word became flesh and made his dwelling among us." (John 1:14). Jesus came from the Father full of grace and truth as a living representation of God Himself. As I read, study, and pour myself into the life of Jesus I grow in my understanding that Jesus, the Living Word, came so that mankind could know the Father. And when I get to know Jesus, I also get to know the one who sent Him-the eternal, all-wise, all-knowing, all-powerful and everlasting God.

Jesus is also known as bread from heaven sent as eternal nourishment for our souls. Not only did He become a source of eternal life for us, but the Words He spoke, and the entirety of the Bible for that matter, continues to nourish us daily as new creatures in Christ.

- Jesus said in John 6:63, "The words I have spoken to you are *spirit and they are life.*" (italics added)

- He said that man does not live on bread alone but on every Word that comes from the mouth of God. (Matthew 4:4)

We can live our life based off of the Word of God! I have come to realize that the Word of God, and the God of the Word, are enough to satisfy my deepest longings, quench the thirst of my heart, grant peace to my mind, and empower me for godliness day to day. We can truly build our lives upon His Word.

Look at what Jesus concluded about the word of God. My prayer is that you too would embrace this verse as your ultimate conclusion concerning God's word also:

"For heaven and earth will pass away, but my words
will never pass away." (Matthew 24:35)

If Jesus declares that His word will never pass away but stand the test of time through all generations and every season of our lives, then we must allow it to dwell in us richly.

The Riches of His Word—The eternal I.R.A

Colossians 3:16 says, "Let the Word of God dwell in you *richly*" (italics added). There are riches for us far beyond anything we could ever have in this life. It is one thing to have an earthly I.R.A., Individual Retirement Account, which we should all have. But there are no riches this side of heaven that come close to the richness of God's Word made real in our life. I want to provide you with a template for a "spiritual I.R.A." as you spend time in his Word. These three things—information, revelation, and application—are the building blocks to establishing your life on God's Word. This is often the study method I use when I read the Bible, and the one I encourage you to try as well.

- **Information**—When you read a passage in the Bible simply ask yourself, "What does this passage say? What are the important details of the passage? Who did what? What interesting facts does the passage contain?" Information does more than sharpen our Bible trivia skills. Information becomes the starting point for one of the most incredible things that happens when we read the Word of God called *revelation.*

- **Revelation**—Revelation is what I call the "aha moment" you have in your time with God each day. Revelation is a fancy word used to describe whenever God allows us to see how the passage we are reading specifically and individually applies to our lives. Simply put, revelation is when you read the Bible only to find that the Bible is actually reading you! Revelation is also that moment when you sense God speaking to you about something in your life or disclosing something to you about Himself. In this way, revelation is a divine download. No wonder Paul prayed in Ephesians 1:17, "I keep asking that the God of our Lord Jesus Christ, the glorious Father, may give you the Spirit of wisdom and revelation, so that you may know him better." This is one of my life verses because it clearly communicates that the Holy Spirit on the inside of me will open my spiritual eyes to know God better—not just with my head (information), but with my heart (revelation).

- **Application**—However, information and fascinating revelation mean nothing without practical application. In fact Scripture is clear about those who read the Word of God yet do not do what it says. James 1:22-25 says, "Do not merely listen to the word, and so deceive yourselves. Do what it says." So, a good final question to ask at the end of reading your Bible is, "how does this passage apply to me and how can I live it out in my life? What steps can I take today to do what I just read in my Bible?"

Sample I.R.A.–John 1

Information
In this chapter, John tells us that through Christ all things were created and that Jesus was also "with God in the beginning." He calls Jesus "the Word" who became flesh, dwelled among us, and was full of grace and truth. This description of Jesus is powerful!

Revelation
v. 12 says that Jesus came from the Father full of grace and truth. This really hit me hard today because the "truth" side of Jesus comes a lot easier for me than the "grace" side! But the Scripture is clear, Jesus came full of both and I need both grace and truth present in my own life as well.

Application
Today, I am reminded of how much grace and forgiveness God has given me through the cross. There is someone in my life right now that I need to extend grace to and make sure that I am not being so hard on in my thoughts and words. Today, I will not only pray for this person, but will reach out to them and encourage them. I may even need to ask them to forgive me if I have come across as too hard on them!

The Ultimate Result
The result of a life rooted in the Word of God is found in an analogy Jesus gives us in Luke 7:24-27. Read this passage and capture the imagery.

"Therefore, everyone who hears these words of mine and puts them into practice is like a wise man who built his house on the rock. The rain came down, the streams rose, and the winds blew and beat against that house; yet it did not fall, because it had its foundation on the rock. But everyone who hears these words of mine and does not put them into practice is like a foolish man who built his house on sand. The rain came down, the streams rose, and the winds blew and beat against that house, and it fell with a great crash."

Jesus is clear. Those who read and build their life on His word will endure any of the severe trials and storms that may come against them. But those who fail to do so are in danger of experiencing a great crash in any area of life not under the authority of God and His Word. Here's one more passage that sums up God's call for us to build our lives on His Word:

Psalm 1:1-3 Blessed is the one who does not walk in step with the wicked or stand in the way that sinners take or sit in the company of mockers, 2 but whose delight is in the law of the Lord, and who meditates on his law day and night. 3 That person is like a tree planted by streams of water, which yields its fruit in season and whose leaf does not wither– whatever they do prospers.

Let's learn to position ourselves near the streams of water by becoming people of the Word who are in touch with the Holy Spirit. Let's not wither spiritually, but let's build our lives upon the good book, the Living Word, the Holy Bible.

Conclusion

Allow me to conclude as I began–I love the Word of God and hunger for it daily. I have discovered the more I devour His Word, the more His Word only deepens this hunger and whets my appetite for more of Him. I don't know about you but I'm ready to invest a little more time into a spiritual I.R.A that yields a daily return for my life. His Word is life, and there is life in His Word. Let's read it, allow God to reveal it, and then do it.

Week 4 Spiritual Workout

- This week, we will start reading through the book of John in the New Testament. Purchase a journal of your choosing. Read chapters 1-3 in the book of John, one chapter a day, and do an IRA for each chapter.

- Share with your mentor or small group some of the insights you gleaned from the first three chapters of John.

- Read the next chapter in this book.

Individual and Small Group Reflection Questions:

1. What is one of your biggest questions about the Bible?

2. What are three key benefits to reading the Word of God on a regular basis?

3. Describe a moment in which you know God spoke to you through His Word.

CHAPTER 5

Inside out Prayer

I grew up in an alcoholic home. My mom was a heavy drinker during the early part of my life. She began drinking before I was born in order to numb the effects of an abusive childhood. She battled severe emotional issues as a result and these issues remained with her as I was growing up. She tried to commit suicide twice when I was young and we spent many days in family counseling. (Note: wait until we get to chapter 13 and I tell you the amazing story of how she came to know Christ!)

Out of the guilt she felt for all she was battling with, she decided to institute a family prayer time around the breakfast table each morning to try and bring a sense of peace to our family. She hadn't even accepted Christ into her life personally at this point. She just knew that my sister and I needed some sense of sanity in the midst of turbulent waters. Each morning, my mom closed the prayer time by leading us in the Lord's prayer. I can still close my eyes and hear the three of us reciting Matthew 6:19-30:

"This, then, is how you should pray: "'Our Father in heaven, hallowed be your name, your kingdom come, your will be done, on earth as it is in heaven. Give us today our daily bread. And forgive us our debts, as we also have forgiven our debtors. And lead us not into temptation, but deliver us from the evil one.'

Little did my mom know that God would use those prayers around the kitchen table each morning to cultivate a child-like awe in my heart about the nature of prayer. I became fascinated with the thought of spending time with the God of eternity. We'd say our prayers together in the morning but at night, after I had gone to bed, I would stay up and pray for anything and anybody I thought needed prayer. And when I say anything, I mean anything. I would pray over everything from our dogs and cats (by name of course) to the emotional issues of my home and family. I even assigned prayers to the different persons of the Trinity. God the Father got the big prayer requests, God the Son got the smaller ones, and God the Holy Spirit got all the leftovers.

My theology was a bit off, but my heart was in the right place. And now, after all these years as a Christian, I am still in awe of a God who wants to spend time with me. I have often echoed the words of Jesus' first disciples who would often overhear Him speaking to His heavenly Father and say, "Lord teach us to pray." (Luke 11:1). And that is what I hope this chapter offers—a teaching on effective prayer.

Prayer as a Priority
Mark 1:35 says, "Very early in the morning, while it was still dark, Jesus got up, left the house and went off to a solitary place, where he prayed." The habit of Jesus Himself was to withdraw from the hustle and bustle of being the Son of God and find a place to spend time with His heavenly father. If Jesus needed this time, then certainly so do we! It was a priority to Him, and it must be a priority to us as well. Have you truly made time with God a priority yet? As a night owl, I hate to highlight this part of the verse, but did you notice when Jesus spent time with the father? Yep. Very early in the morning. Time with God is certainly worth waking up for, but whatever the time of day we choose, we must embrace this time as a non-negotiable priority for our lives.

Determine a Place
An effective prayer life starts, as it did for Jesus, with a designated time and designated solitary place. This time is often referred to as a "Quiet

Time" because it is the time during your day that you put aside all the distractions clamoring for your attention and are alone with God. This can be at your kitchen table before everyone else gets up in the morning or at your office before you take that first phone call, respond to that first email, or update your first status of the day on Facebook. Of course, you can spend time with God on your way to work or at night after everyone else goes to bed, or any other time when you can set aside some quiet moments in your day. But for me, as mentioned above, I have found that the morning time is the best time to seek God with a clear mind that is not yet cluttered with all the details of my day. Time with Jesus first thing in the morning produces a peace within me to guard my heart from whatever life may throw at me that day. It also instills in me a proper outlook on life for the day. For me, I take my kids to school and then spend time with God from 8-9am at my office before everyone else gets there. When will you spend time with God and where will you spend time with Him from this point forward? Let's look now at some specifics concerning our time with God.

Let's pray like Jesus!
Look once again at the Lord's prayer. Read it slowly and then ponder deeply on it for a moment. Matthew 6:9-13:

"This, then, is how you should pray: "'Our Father in heaven, hallowed be your name, your kingdom come, your will be done, on earth as it is in heaven. Give us today our daily bread. And forgive us our debts, as we also have forgiven our debtors. And lead us not into temptation, but deliver us from the evil one.'

Jesus starts off by saying "This, then, is how you should pray." Jesus then gives us four key insights. They happen to spell out the acronym P.R.A.Y. (In the spirit of full disclosure, this acronym has been around forever. I'm not sure who came up with it but I'm glad they did!)

P—Praise! ("Hallowed be thy name")
This one is key! Starting off your time with God by praising Him. Praise is giving thanks and adoration to God for who He is and all that He has done for us out of His goodness and grace. By praising the Lord first, you can begin to free your mind from all the clutter of life and silence

the lies that Satan tends to whisper to your soul. Early on in my walk with the Lord, I learned to open up the book of Psalms, which is a book in the Bible that is full of praise and read one Psalm out loud to start off my time with Him. After reading it out loud, I would put the Psalm into my own words and personalize my praise to God. I still do this often and would encourage you to give it a try.

R–Repent ("Forgive us our trespasses")

It is important to acknowledge any sin or shortcomings before God during our prayer time. Doing so allows us to experience the sense of peace that comes whenever we are forgiven and clean before His presence. 1 John 1:9 says, "If we confess our sins, he is faithful and just and will forgive us our sins and purify us from all unrighteousness." Allow the Holy Spirit to survey your heart and if there is anything that needs to be dealt with, simply acknowledge that before God with humility. Confess it, receive God's grace, ask Him to help you, and move on in the freedom of His forgiveness.

A–Ask ("Give us this day our daily bread")

This is where you simply ask God to perform His will in the different areas of your life. Ask honestly and openly. God can handle your transparency and would have you come before Him only in this way. One thing I do to help me make sure that I am praying over all the key areas in my life is assign a different category of life to each day of the week and focus on that category during my prayer time. For example, on Mondays, I always pray for my family. On Tuesdays, I pray over the staff at my church. On Wednesdays, I pray over the needs of people within my church. On Thursdays, I pray for my own relationship with the Lord as well as my growth and development as a husband and a father. On Fridays, I pray over my dreams and hopes for the future. On Saturdays and Sundays, I pray over anything I might have missed during the week or anything the Holy Spirit lays on my heart. Assigning a different category to each day of the week can help make praying easier and help you create consistency in presenting your requests to God.

Y–Yield ("Thy kingdom come, thy will be done")

Yielding simply means acknowledging that you desire for the will of God to be done in your life and then listening for His voice in the midst of your prayer time. Silence your thoughts before His presence and listen. The more you do, the more you will begin to sense how and when God speaks to you and this becomes very, very exciting. One thing you may want to do is record what you feel like God is speaking to you or what you learned through His Word that day in a journal of some kind. Journaling is a powerful spiritual exercise.

Putting it all together

Last chapter, I gave you an acronym to follow in your time with the word– the I.R.A Bible study plan. Now, I have just given you another acronym to follow regarding your time in prayer–P.R.A.Y. If you were to put all of this together in one quiet time with the Lord, it would look like the following. Note: This could all be done within 30 minutes or less a day!

- Start off with your quiet time by reading one Psalm out loud and then spend a few minutes praising God. Invite God to scan your heart and life for anything that may not be pleasing to Him.

- Turn in your Bible to whatever book you are currently reading and ask God to give you a Spirit of wisdom and revelation as you read it (Ephesians 1:17). In order to avoid feeling overwhelmed read just one chapter or passage a day.

- As you read one chapter or passage, have a journal handy and look for a point of information, a point of revelation, and a point of application within that text. Jot down 1-2 sentences or bullet points under the headings "information", "revelation", and "application" in your journal.

- Thank God for what He showed you and ask Him to help you apply it to your life.

- Next, ask Him for whatever needs you are bringing before Him today. Pray over your category of the day.

- After making your requests known to God, take a moment and simply yield to Him. Sit quietly for a minute and just be with God, listening intently. Write down anything you feel like God may be speaking to you and then close with a brief prayer of thanksgiving.

If you don't like using acronyms and journals to guide your quiet time, then find what works for you. These are simply suggestions that you can glean from to help you grow. The important thing is to open your Bible on a regular basis and start talking with God.

That's it. That is what a good daily spiritual workout with God could look like. Make it your own. Allow the Holy Spirit to shape this time for you personally. But get that spiritual muscle moving!

Conclusion

Sometimes I will lay in bed at night and speak with God the way I did as a child. Yes, I still have a quiet time much earlier in the day. But every once in a while, I return to my roots where my prayer life originated and lay in bed at night just talking with God. My prayer is that you and I will fall in love once again with the very thought that the God of the universe desires to spend time with us, listens to every word we say, and will actually speak back through the Holy Spirit within us.

Week 5 Spiritual Workout

This week, your assignment is to come up with a different category of prayer for each day of the week to guide your daily prayer time. Go ahead now and write out a possible plan for each day of the week:

Monday:

Tuesday:

Wednesday:

Thursday:

Friday:

- Secondly, continue with the next three chapters in the book of John (chapters 4-6). Do an IRA for at least one of these chapters and practice praying using the P.R.A.Y acronym.

- Read the next chapter in this book.

Reflection Questions For Individual or Small Group Use

1. What time of day will you commit to spend time in God's Word and pray? Where (as in the actual physical location) will you have your quiet times?

2. What aspect of the P.R.A.Y acronym seems more likely to come easy for you? The hardest?

3. Do you believe God wants to speak to you regularly? If so, what are some things you can do to ensure you continue to hear His voice?

CHAPTER 6

Inside-Out Church Attendance

When I was twelve or thirteen years old, my best friend Chris and I were determined to become professional bodybuilders. (I chuckle even writing that first sentence.) We joined a gym and our parents graciously took us as much as we wanted to go. It wasn't the highest end gym mind you. It was a sweatshop full of metal plates and muscle heads. We looked at these guys in amazement, determined to transform our scrawny bodies into beasts. (Chuckle again.)

The guy who worked at the front desk was named Tony. He was a big dude. Very big. We asked Tony for some pointers and he actually turned out to be a pretty nice guy. The one piece of advice he gave us on our first day was simply this: "Make sure you spot each other."

You probably know what spotting is during weightlifting. During a bench press, the spotter stands over the bar as you lower the weight to your chest and then press it upwards. The spotter makes sure your form is right and is there to catch the bar should it become too heavy, which could result in serious injury. They are also there to encourage you to safely push past your limit in order to build muscle.

We need spotters in the natural for a physical workout and we need spotters as well for our spiritual workout. Hebrews 10:24-25 tells us:

"And let us consider how we may spur one another on toward love and good deeds, not giving up meeting together, as some are in the habit of doing, but encouraging one another— and all the more as you see the Day approaching."

The writer of Hebrews tells us that meeting together in a corporate worship service helps us to spur one another on toward spiritual growth. In other words, our local church and the fellow believers we are doing life with "spot" us—they guide us in our spiritual formation, help protect us from danger, and even push us beyond the limits we've placed on ourselves so we can grow spiritually. However, he also tells us that many are in the habit of neglecting this vitally important spiritual discipline.

This chapter outlines three reasons we should continue to attend church, meet with one another, and become personally connected to other believers. In short, through the local church we are empowered, equipped, and encouraged. And we need all three!

Through the church I am empowered
I have always loved what Jesus said in John 4:24. "God is spirit, and his worshipers must worship in Spirit and in truth." We are called to worship God together in a local church. As we do so, the Holy Spirit is present and reveals to us more and more of the truth of who God is through our worship. Our connection to God and others is strengthened and we are empowered in our faith. Allow me to illustrate this from my own journey of church attendance.

The very first church I was a part of right after becoming a Christian was Abundant Life Church on the outskirts of Columbus, GA. It was a small non-denominational church whose pastor, John Knox, was a phenomenal Bible teacher. He continuously taught us about the character and nature of God the Father and who we are as His children. It was in this church that I began to understand my identity in Christ, and what it means to have a healthy and Biblical self-esteem. I also learned how to receive and walk in God's forgiveness. I was connecting with the Holy Spirit through this man's teaching because He was bringing a word that was timely for the season of life I was currently experiencing. Every message seemed like it was just for me.

This may certainly not be the case every time you listen to your pastor deliver God's Word on Sunday mornings. However, I have discovered something powerful. If I am growing as a Christian and I am hungry for the Word of God, the Holy Spirit will take any teaching and any sermon and tailor make it just for me. I love Hebrews 4:12 which says, "For the word of God is living and active."

God's Word is living and active! The more I read it, study it, and meditate on it in my own personal time with the Lord, the more I will tune into the teaching I absorb through my church whether it be Sunday school lessons, Sunday morning sermons, Wednesday night teachings, or small group curriculum. This might sound harsh, but Christians who tend to complain about "not being fed" in church are usually not feeding themselves throughout the week! But as I feast on God's Word Monday through Saturday, I find something incredible starts to happen. I start to experience the Holy Spirit connecting dots between what I am studying and reading on my own throughout the week and what I hear on Sunday mornings or during other discipleship opportunities my church offers. Remember, Jesus is the author of our faith, and He loves to deepen His connection with us by cultivating a synergy between what we are learning individually and corporately. When this synergy happens, the combined effect produces unstoppable growth for the believer and an unbreakable connection with the Father.

The next church I attended was in Columbus, Ga. This particular church was strong in worship and prayer. In fact, on Sunday nights, at the end of each message, the pastor would allow us to receive prayer at the front of the church. I used to love this time because I knew that if I would stand in one particular place at the front of the church these little old ladies would pray for me. And when I say they prayed; I mean they prayed! You see, these ladies had lived through the Great Depression and several different wars. They raised children on their own while their husbands were away serving in the military or working tirelessly around the clock to provide for their families. And through it all, these ladies had learned to cling to the power and strength of Jesus Christ and that power showed up mightily when they prayed. I could sense the Lord in their soft hands on my back and I could hear their rock-solid faith as they prayed. I could feel the strength of the Lord flow through them as I listened to their simple yet powerful pleas for God to keep me close to Him and grow me into the man I was destined to become. I still get chills when I think back to those times. I am convinced that we need to strive to become more like the "little old ladies" and "little old men" who know how to pray with faith and who allow the Spirit of God to empower others through them.

I share all of this to bring home the point Jesus made in Matthew 18:20, "For where two or three gather in my name, there am I with them." Jesus makes an incredible statement in this passage. He says that when just two or three gather in His name He is there in their midst. Did you catch that? When a group of unified Christians gather in His name, to honor Him and learn about Him, He himself dwells among them. He is there. He is there in His power. He is there in His peace. He is there in His authority and dominion. He is present as the bondage breaker, the life-builder, and the promise fulfiller. He is there in His victory over the devil and the works of darkness. If He is present in this way when just two or three gathers in His name, imagine what a corporate church setting could be like!

Through the church I am equipped

After the little old ladies prayed for me one last time, I went off to college at the University of Georgia. My roommate and I were looking for something to do on the first Friday night we were in Athens, our new home city. We drove by a church that had one of those good ole fashion marquees that said something to the affect of "college hangout-free food." I pulled into the parking lot, thinking we had nothing to lose, but there weren't very many cars where the party was to be held. I turned the car around to leave and all of the sudden this guy began to chase our car down. His name was Michael Miller. He was the campus pastor of a college ministry and this church was his home church. They were allowing him to host this get together to reach new college students. Long story short, from that night forward, I never attended another church for the next ten years. In fact, I would eventually become the youth pastor of that very church and serve under the man whom I now call my lifetime pastor, Mark Northcutt. It was in this church that I endured a very difficult wilderness season and it was because of this church I survived it. It was also through that campus ministry connected to this local church that I met my wife. All, I repeat all, of this took place because of one man who chased me down in a parking lot on a Friday night.

Allow me to chase a squirrel for a moment, but we need Christians and churches who are willing to chase people down again. We need to call our brothers and sisters who seem to be slipping spiritually and refuse to allow them to be picked off by the devil on our watch. We need to encourage them to remain strong, help them refuse a spirit of isolation, and help them refocus their minds and hearts on the things of God. And we need to remind them of the significance and value they bring to the life of the church. This is exactly what Michael Miller did for me. He took me under his wing and discipled me. He was my small group leader and an accountability partner. And he also equipped me to take my God-given gifts to the next level.

It was through my involvement with this campus ministry that I felt a call toward evangelism. In fact, it was Michael who first taught me how to share my faith. As he was doing so, something ignited in my spirit. I just knew I was gifted to do this and to teach others to do the same. As a result, I started an evangelism team with a group of my peers. After a season as a youth pastor, I then traveled the nation for eleven years telling people about Jesus as an evangelist. I started a school of missions and evangelism for young people who desired to travel and tell others about Christ in a variety of different contexts (www.mymissionsjourney.com). I also wrote an entire church campaign to empower churches to present Christ to their communities (www.reachthecity.com). All of this took place because of a local church body equipping me for ministry. It was this season of equipping that caused one domino after another to fall towards a greater destiny for my life.

I'm not sure what the dominoes will be for you, and please don't compare your journey to mine. I share my story as an example of the importance of being equipped for whatever God's calling for you may be. The job of pastors and the church is to equip the body for the work of the ministry. Your job is to embrace the process of being equipped. This will cause you to feel connected to something bigger than yourself and enable you to use your God given strengths for the eternal things that really matter. Being used by God, regardless of how big or small our efforts may seem, will satisfy us in a way nothing else can. When you allow God to use you, the dominoes of destiny for your own life will fall forward into a future of deeper meaning and greater vision. We will explore being used by God more in the fourth section of this book, but for now I encourage you to get involved on a greater level in your local church. You will be blessed and so will they!

Through the church I am encouraged

Lastly, the local church provides us the encouragement we all need in a world full of discouraging times. This might take place through the friendliness of our church family greeting us on Sunday mornings with a smile or through the message and worship that seem to speak directly to our circumstances. This might take place during a prayer time in the service where someone stands with you and prays with you concerning the needs of your life. This might take place as we laugh together at the Mexican Restaurant (yum!) after service. And this might take place as you serve together in nursery, play golf together on Saturday after-noons, grab coffee together before the kids get out of school, or as you spend time with each other in a small group on a Tuesday night. The encouragement we receive through our time with each other can take place in a variety of different ways. But there is nothing like the life that is imparted to our soul as we fellowship with one another in the body of Christ.

Let me conclude with an even stronger point about our need to fellowship with each other through the local church. Look again at the verse at the beginning of the chapter that I italicized, Hebrews 10:24-25. "And let us consider how we may spur one another on toward love and good deeds, not giving up meeting together, as some are in the habit of doing, but encouraging one another—and all the more as you see the Day approaching." We are to remain connected with each other *all the more*. We need more fellowship and encouragement and not less, which is the current trend of today's churchgoer. Secondly, we need to do so in light of what the Bible refers to as the Day approaching. This Day is the second coming of Christ for the church. As this Day approaches, the Scripture is clear that the devil will continue to increase his deception against the church, the fallen nature of the world will become more evident, and false doctrine will prevail against many. The writer of Hebrews is clear. In the days we are in, and in the days that are to come, we are stronger together. May we refuse to neglect the important spiritual discipline of attending a local church and may we be encouraged and strengthened by our fellowship with one another.

Conclusion

There are many reasons why church attendance is declining in America. But the reasons to remain connected to each other through a local church certainly outweigh them all. Through the local body I am empowered with the Spirit of God and the truth of His Word. I am equipped to live for a larger purpose by discovering and using my God-given gifts, talents, and abilities. And I find encouragement and strength to remain strong in the day and time I in which I am living. Let's embrace our local church and allow this connection to only strengthen our walk with the Lord that much more.

Week 6 Spiritual Workout

- This week, your assignment is to recommit yourself to a local church. If you do not have a church home, then I encourage you to embrace a four-week challenge. Don't miss church for the next four weeks in a row—no matter what. If you are not involved in a church, spend the next four weeks visiting a few churches in which you may be interested. Narrow down the search over the next 6-8 weeks and commit yourself to a local church.

- Continue with the next three chapters in the book of John (chapters 7-9). Do an IRA for at least one of these chapters and practice praying using the PRAY acronym.

- Read the next chapter in this book.

Reflection Questions For Individual Or Small Group Use

1. How faithful are you to attending church regularly? What are some reasons for people struggling in the area of faithful church attendance? From your point of view, what are the three most important qualities a local church must have?

2. John Knox. Michael Miller. Mark Northcutt. In this chapter I intentionally used the names of men who had a great impact on my walk with God personally. I described on some level what God was doing in me during those seasons of my life. Take a moment and do the same. Reflect on and share about the people and churches that have impacted you the most thus far. Describe what you feel God did in you or for you during those seasons. Now, describe who is currently influencing your walk with God the most, the one thing God is teaching you through your church, and what you desire God to do in you as you remain committed to doing life with others.

3. Who is one person in your life that needs to be "chased down" in this season? How will you pursue them this week?

SECTION 3
OFFERING GOD YOUR EVERYTHING

Welcome to section 3 of our spiritual workout! In the previous section, we moved into the first phase of our workout. Remember, there are four different muscle groups we are seeking to build that comprise the CORE of our faith:

C-Connect with God

O-Offer God Everything

R-Release Your Ministry

E-Engage In Personal Outreach and Missions

In this section, we dive into discovering what it really means to Offer God Our Everything. Romans 12:1-2 will serve as our memory verse as we move through this section.

*Therefore, I urge you brothers, in view of God's mercy, to **offer your bodies** as living sacrifices, holy and pleasing to God-this is your spiritual act of worship. Do not conform any longer to the pattern of this world, but be transformed by the renewing of your mind. Then you will be able to test and approve what God's will is-his good, pleasing and perfect will (bold added).*

In this passage, Paul states the truth of our second CORE discipline clearly. We are to offer God our *everything*, our very lives for the sake of His glory. In fact, when Paul says, "this is your spiritual act of worship," this phrase can also be translated "this is your reasonable act of worship." In other words, the only reasonable thing for us to do in light of everything God has done for us is for us to offer everything to Him in complete and total obedience.

Desiring to live a life pleasing to Him, coupled with a willingness to lay everything down for His sake, should become an automatic response as we grow in our understanding of who He is and what He has done. This is a challenging thought no doubt, but is made both possible and desirable through the work of the Holy Spirit in our hearts.

So, let's move into the next section of our discipleship together with our minds set on moving into a deeper relationship with the Lord. Let us recommit to offering our everything to God!

CHAPTER 7

Inside Out Obedience

Remember from chapter two how we discussed the Holy Spirit working on the inside of us in order that we may act according to His good purpose? Well, I'll never forget the season of my life when the Holy Spirit impressed upon my heart to give up secular music. I am not one of those guys who believes all secular music is necessarily bad or sinful. But a lot of the music I listened to early on in my walk with the Lord was a bad influence on my young Christian mind. At first, I argued with God, "But God, not all of my music is bad. I mean, Bon Jovi even sings the song Living on A Prayer! How can that be bad!!??"

Have you ever done this? Have you ever tried to argue with the God of the universe? Trust me. That never works out too well. As I processed what I knew God was asking me to do, the more it made sense. Not that everything He asks us to do has to make sense in order for us to obey Him. But I began to realize how contradictory it was for me to sing Def Leopard's song, Pour Some Sugar On Me, on the way to youth group! (Okay, I'm totally revealing my age and style of music choice with this chapter).

I argued with the Holy Spirit over this issue for a week and I finally decided to take a radical step of obedience. I took all of my cassette tapes (you younger people can google what those are), went out to my backyard, and proceeded to smash every one of them with a hammer. Little did I know that this act was an expression of what is known in the Bible as sanctification.

Sanctification is a Biblical term used to describe the role of the Holy Spirit making us more and more like Jesus, which is, after all, the ultimate goal of our faith. And to this end the Holy Spirit works within us deeply and thoroughly in order to prune away anything that does not glorify God. Paul states it this way in 1 Thessalonians 5:23,

> "May God himself, the God of peace, sanctify you through and through. May your whole spirit, soul and body be kept blameless at the coming of our Lord Jesus Christ."

The Holy Spirit sanctifies us, making us more like Jesus...through and through! Every thought, every attitude, every behavior. He makes us more like Jesus from the inside out.

Within a week or two of taking a sledgehammer to my cassette tapes, someone approached me and said, "I feel impressed to give this to you." She put my very first praise and worship tape in my hand. Since I had nothing else to listen to at this point, I immediately put this tape into my walk-man (again, use google) and listened to it night after night laying in my bed before falling asleep. And it was in that season, listening to this tape over and over again, that God gave me visions of preaching and writing, which was my call to the ministry. If I hadn't offered God my everything in that season, I could have potentially missed or at least delayed the call of God on my life.

I learned three valuable lessons in those early days of my faith that have stayed with me to this day:

- When God tells us "no," it is because he has a greater "yes" for our life.

- Christianity isn't just about the absence of evil. It is about the presence of good (and God) in our lives.

- It's impossible for Jesus to be Lord and for us to tell him "No." Think about it. If Jesus is truly our Lord, the only response to our Lord when He speaks to us is "Yes.": If we tell Him "no" concerning an area of our lives, then we haven't surrendered fully to His Lordship, hindering the process of sanctification.

These deep lessons led me to conclude that obedience to God is ultimately for my good and that God wrote every command with my very best interest in mind. When the Holy Spirit asked me to give up my secular music in that season, it wasn't because every secular song is necessarily "bad." It was just that God had something better for me to pursue during that time of my life. And it wasn't that He was trying to take away all my fun. It was that He was trying to fulfill me with something much more meaningful. Aren't you grateful that Jesus didn't come to take away our fun and bore us to death, but to bless us with the abundant life He made available to us through His death and resurrection? I sure am. And we experience this abundant life when Jesus becomes our all in all.

Jesus, Our All In All

We should go all in for God because He went all in for us. We should hold nothing back from Him because He held nothing back from us. And we should give Him our everything because He gave everything for us. In fact, we really need to look at our CORE verse again, Philippians 2:12-13. The fact is, Paul starts off Philippians 2:12 with the word "therefore."

"Therefore, my dear friends, as you have always obeyed—not only in my presence, but now much more in my absence—continue to work out your salvation with fear and trembling, for it is God who works in you to will and to act according to His good purpose" (italics added).

I was taught as a new Christian that whenever you see the word "therefore" in the Bible, you need to read the preceding verses and see what it is "there for!" And check out the incredible passage that precedes the command to work out our salvation. Philippians 2:5-11 says

"Your attitude should be the same as that of Christ Jesus: Who, being in very nature of God, did not consider equality with God something to be grasped, but made himself nothing, taking the very nature of a servant, being made in human likeness. And being found in appearance as a man, he humbled himself and became obedient to death—even death on a cross! Therefore God exalted him to the highest place and gave him the name that is above every name, that at the name of Jesus every knee should bow, in heaven and on earth and under the earth, and every tongue confess that Jesus Christ is Lord, to the glory of God the Father."

I get overwhelmed with awe by this passage of Scripture because it describes Jesus--the one the Bible also declares as the First and the Last, the Beginning and the End, the Firstborn of all creation, and the One through whom all things were created and all things hold together—as the one who emptied Himself of all his heavenly glory in order to come to this earth to die on the cross for my sins. The one who was always worthy of being served and worshipped took the nature of a servant to walk with man and seek and save those who were lost. He humbled himself to the Father's will, to the point of dying an excruciating death on the cross as He took our sin and the punishment we rightly deserve on His back. God truly made him who had no sin to be sin for us, so that in him we might become the righteousness of God! (2 Corinthians 5:21) Jesus surrendered Himself to the plan of the Father and offered Himself for us—holding nothing back!

But of course, the story of Jesus going all in doesn't stop at the cross. God then exerted His power in Jesus' lifeless body and resurrected Him, bringing Him back to life so that we might have eternal life. He then ascended back into heaven and sat down at the right hand of the Father. And according to what we just read in Philippians 2, one day, whether it is on this side of heaven or at the final judgement of man, every knee will bow, and every tongue confess that this same Jesus is truly Lord of all! Paul then pivots and states the verse this book is centered on, "Therefore (because of His Lordship), continue to work out your salvation with fear and trembling." In other words, with deep respect and reverential awe of Jesus who is Lord over the universe, continue to make Him your Lord over all areas of your life.

Jesus Our One and Only

John 3:16 is perhaps the most popular verse in all of the Bible because within it is the central truth of our faith. Read it slowly and pay attention to what I have italicized, "For God so loved the world that *He gave His one and only* Son that whosoever believes in Him shall not perish but have everlasting life." Did you catch that? God gave His one and only Son for us. And why? So that ultimately Jesus would become our one and only! Let me say it again:

God gave us His one and only Son so that Jesus would become our one and only God.

In the Old Testament the people of God were commanded to have no other gods before Him. (Exodus 20:3). In the New Testament Jesus is questioned concerning the most important command in the Bible to obey. Listen to his response in Matthew 22:37,

"'Love the Lord your God with all your heart and with all your soul and with all your mind."

Jesus declared that every command of Christianity is ultimately summed up with just one command—to love God in all things. And what is the highest expression of our love for Him? Obedience.

John 14:23 "If anyone loves me, he will obey my teaching."

There is no true love for God apart from obedience. And remember, as we said at the start of this chapter, offering every aspect of our lives to God in total obedience is the only reasonable response we can have to Jesus offering Himself for us. When our motive for obedience is love for God, our willingness to obey God's Word and what the Holy Spirit prompts us to do becomes easier and is an expression of worship from the heart. Let's end this particular chapter with a heartfelt prayer.

Conclusion

Father God, I thank you that you sent your one and only Son so that you might become my one and only God. Jesus help me to love you and follow you from the inside out and thank you for the Holy Spirit who helps me to do just that. Lord, I recommit myself to you again as Lord of my life.

I offer you my everything and commit to withhold nothing. Thank you that your Lordship is the best thing for my life because it prunes me, protects me, and preserves the awareness of your presence in my life. Thank you that you have called me your friend. Today I once again call you Lord. In Jesus' name. Amen.

Week 7 Spiritual Workout

- Select one of two challenges for this week:
  - **Smash Challenge**—Pray through whether or not there is anything in your life that is getting between you and God. This could be an action or an attitude. This could be a bad habit or a way of thinking. Invite the Holy Spirit to help you surrender that area of your life to the Lord. And then do whatever is necessary to take a step of obedience in that area. It could be smashing a cassette tape (ok, deleting a playlist) or it could be asking someone to forgive you for something you did. But whatever your decision, tell some-one you trust. Accountability is key to helping a permanent transformation take place in that area of your life.

  - **Fasting**—Fast a "good thing." What I mean by this is to give up something for a week that isn't necessarily bad, but a potential distraction in your walk with Jesus. Social media is a great example.

- Continue with the next three chapters in the book of John (chapters 10-12). Do an IRA for at least one of these chapters and practice praying using the PRAY acronym.
- Read the next chapter in this book.

Reflection Questions For Individual Or Small Group Use

1. Is there any area in your life in which you are having difficulty surrendering to God and obeying Him fully? Have you ever felt like the Holy Spirit has asked you to surrender or give something up? What was this experience like for you? What was the fruit of your decision?

2. How does obedience and love go hand in hand for the believer?

3. Are you truly convinced that obedience is a good thing? Do you really believe that God has your best interest at heart when he tells you "no?" And do you really believe that God tells us "no" because He always has a better "yes" in mind?

CHAPTER 8

Inside-Out Victory

My Story

As I mentioned in chapter 3, I grew up in an alcoholic home with an atmosphere that could easily lend itself to depression. By the time I graduated from elementary school at the ripe age of 12 years old, individual and family therapy had become a regular part of my weekly routine. In the seventh grade, I found myself in counseling for suicidal thoughts. I battled discouragement, depression, and other addictions as well.

Why do I share such deeply personal things with you? Because I know that if God can help me, He can help you. If He can help me to walk in wholeness emotionally and to walk in freedom over sin, I am convinced He can do it for anybody—including you!

Galatians 5:1 says, "It is for freedom that Christ has set us free."

Jesus said in John 8:31, "If you hold to my teaching, you are really my disciples. Then you will know the truth, and the truth will set you free."

In this chapter, I want to outline some teaching from the Word of God that leads to our transformation and lasting freedom. The first two of them are very spiritual in nature while the other three of them are very practical in nature. Let's jump into the first one, but please, keep reading through to the end of the chapter!

Finding Freedom Through The Fear Of The Lord

I am a quote guy. I love quotes and I love it when God gives me little quips and witty sayings to help me remember some deep truths. Here is one of the first quotes I learned as a Christian:

"If you don't take sin seriously, you will seriously sin."

Ouch! I'm not even sure who said it, but this quote still slaps spiritual sense into my soul to this very day. And it also leads me to highlight a few more words from Philippians 2:12-13. Look at the four words I have italicized for you.

"Therefore, my dear friends, as you have always obeyed—not only in my presence, but now much more in my absence—continue to work out your salvation *with fear and trembling*, for it is God who works in you to will and to act according to His good purpose." (italics added)

Did you catch it? Paul says to work out our salvation "with fear and trembling." These four words are the elephant in the room nobody wants to talk about when it comes to this passage. But these words are the very first key to our freedom. We must learn to fear the Lord. Look at another verse worth committing to memory:

> Proverbs 1:7 The fear of the Lord is the beginning of
> knowledge, but fools despise wisdom and discipline.

To have the fear of the Lord is to embrace an attitude of deep respect for the Holiness of God marked by reverence, awe, and honor. It also means to love what God loves and to hate what God hates—which is sin. Think about sin for a minute:

- Sin is what originally separated mankind from God in the first place.

- Sin is the very reason why sickness and death are now a part of our world.

- Sin is the source of all grief, injustice, and oppression in the earth.

- Sin is perpetuated by the deception of the devil whose only motive is to steal, kill, and destroy.

Sin stinks. I don't know any other way to say it. And if we don't take sin seriously by fearing the Lord, we are more likely to seriously sin. But if we commit ourselves to fearing Him, living in awe and reverence of who He is, the Holy Spirit can then continue to lead us into greater places of freedom. Think of it this way. The foundation of our freedom is the fear of the Lord.

The Grace Of God

It may seem odd to go straight from the fear of God to the grace of God. However, I believe these two spiritual dynamics are two sides of the same coin called freedom. We need both equally. Two verses come to mind:

- Lamentations 3:22-23 "Because of the Lord's great love we are not consumed, for his compassions never fail. They are new every morning; great is your faithfulness."

- Titus 2:11-12 "For the grace of God has appeared that offers salvation to all people. It teaches us to say 'No' to ungodliness and worldly passions, and to live self-controlled, upright and godly lives in this present age,"

Every morning when we wake up, God's mercy provides us with a fresh new start. He doesn't hold yesterday's mistakes and sins over our heads. In fact, the very moment we confess our sin, he forgives us and makes us clean. 1 John 1:9 says, "If we confess our sins, he is faithful and just and will forgive us our sins and purify us from all unrighteousness." This verse even applies to those areas of our life that we seem to struggle with time and time again. If we are struggling on a daily basis to overcome something, yet our hearts are sincere and repentant, he proves Himself as being slow to anger, rich in love, and continuously forgiving us as we are being transformed into His likeness.

But notice something about God's grace itself. It is a teacher. The grace of God, abiding in us through the presence of the Holy Spirit, steers us away from evil and toward that which is good. The grace of God is also His divine enablement at work within us through the Holy Spirit. As we spend time with God and offer ourselves to Him, His grace at work on the inside of us becomes our supernatural source to stay free from sin.

Now that we have discussed the two big spiritual paradigms to our freedom, the fear of the Lord and His grace, allow me to give you 3 quick practical ways to walk in freedom.

Embrace an Accountable Relationship

Here is another key verse every believer should memorize.

> James 5:16 "Therefore, confess your sins to each other
> and pray for each other so that you may be healed."

This is a powerful verse and I want to turn your attention to one word within it; healed. When we confess to others, we are healed. Think about that. It might seem to be a bit unusual but here is the punchline.

When we confess to God, we are forgiven. But when we confess to others, we are healed.

And here's why. The blood of Jesus alone is what cleanses us from sin (1 John 1:7), but when we are willing to expose our sin to people we trust, something amazing happens. Sin loses its grip and power. Think of it this way:

> What we keep in the darkness grows, but
> what we bring into the light dies!

That's a dynamic principle of the Christian life. When we are willing to be vulnerable and transparent with people we trust, sin loses its grip on us. We begin to discover that our vulnerability empowers our victory and our transparency is the starting point to our turning point. I once heard another final quote that I want to share with you. Often times, you will hear the phrase, "Get right with God." And that is certainly true but so is this:

We will never get right until we get real.

So, who is that one person in your life with whom you can get real? Have you confessed your sin struggles to him/her? Have you asked them to hold you accountable? Here is the second practical principle to walking in freedom:

Walk Wisely

Listen to this verse:

> Proverbs 28:26 He who trusts in himself is a fool,
> but he who walks in wisdom is kept safe.

We must learn to walk wisely through this life. Walking in wisdom can take on many different aspects. Proverbs 4:23-27 sums it up best because it outlines three practical ways to walk in wisdom but does so in light of protecting our heart. Read the passage and look at the three domains of life in which we must walk wisely:

"Above all else, guard your heart, for it is the wellspring of life Put away perversity from your mouth; keep corrupt talk far from your lips. Let your eyes look straight ahead; fix your gaze directly before you. Make level paths for your feet and take only ways that are firm. Do not swerve to the right or the left; keep your foot from level."

Here is a good checklist for wisdom based on this passage:

- Our mouths (v.24). We are to put perversity away from our mouths. Scripture says the power of life and death is in the tongue (Proverbs 18:21). We must ask ourselves, what kind of speech is coming from our lips? Life or death? Blessing or cursing?

- Our eyes– (v.25). We are to fix our gaze straight ahead. We are to keep our eyes on Jesus and keep ourselves pure by only looking at things that honor Him. What kinds of things am I looking at and what am I allowing my eyes to see? Monitoring what we allow to cross the threshold of our eyes is crucial to walking in freedom.

- Our feet– (v.26). We are to take ways that are level and firm. Where are our feet taking us? This includes actual physical places that could compromise our purity as well as any area of life in which we are not embracing God's ways. For example, embracing God's principles in the area of finances, opposite sex relationships, and Biblical work ethic are just a few examples of specific areas in which we are to learn and then embrace the ways of God. Are there any of these areas that are shaky and need to be strengthened through obedience?

If I were to add one more, I would add:

- Our company–Who do we hang out with? 1 Corinthians 15:33 says, "bad company corrupts good character." The company we keep often influences the character we have. Don't mistake me here. I absolutely desire that we all spend time with non-Christians and win as many of them to the Lord as we can. However, we must also make sure that we are the ones with the greater influence in the relationship.

Our mouth, our eyes, our feet, and our company. These are all good areas to start with when evaluating whether or not we are walking in wisdom. How are you doing in each of them?

Renew Your Mind With The Help Of The Holy Spirit

Ok, another foundational Bible verse for us is:

Romans 12:2 "Do not conform any longer to the pattern of this world, but be transformed by the renewing of your mind."

The level of freedom in our life is in direct relationship to our thought life. In fact, here is a formula for you to remember:

What I dwell on becomes what I desire and eventually do.

What I mean by this is that whatever I set my mind on will determine the way I feel. And often times, the way I feel will determine the course of my feet (my course of action).

That is why Paul encourages us in Colossians 3:2 to "set our minds on things above, not on earthly things." He also tells us to focus on the things that are true, noble, right, pure, lovely, admirable, and excellent. He tells us simply to "think about such things." (Philippians 4:8) Why? Because what we focus on will determine our feelings, will influence our ability to remain free from sin, and will ultimately influence our faithfulness to God.

With the help of the Holy Spirit, we must learn to take every thought captive and make it obedient to Christ (2 Corinthians 10:5). And as we do so, we will walk in freedom—from the inside out.

Conclusion

Let's end this chapter with a verse from the beginning:

Galatians 5:1 "It is for freedom that Christ has set us free"

Christ Jesus came to this earth that we might be free. He rescued us from the dominion of darkness and brought us into His marvelous light (Colossians 1:13). And He is still the bondage breaker and the great liberator. He is the one who can make us whole regardless of any habit, hurt, or hang up we are currently battling.

The truth is, you and I can walk in freedom, but again, we must learn to:

1. Fear God

2. Understand His Grace

3. Embrace accountability

4. Walk wisely

5. Renew our minds

Spiritual Workout Week 8

- One of the absolute best ways to renew our minds is by not only reading God's word but memorizing it and meditating on it. This week's challenge is to memorize Psalms 1:1-3. But don't just commit it to memory. Ponder and think deeply on it as you do! Now practice writing it out below:

_____

_____

_____

_____

- Continue reading the book of John. Read chapters 13-15 and do at least one IRA for one of the chapters. Practice praying using the PRAY acronym.

- Read chapter 9 in this book.

Reflection Questions For Individual Or Small Group Use

1. Which of the five concepts above (fear of God, grace of God, accountability, walking wisely, renewing your mind) are easy for you to grasp and live out? Which are harder?

2. Who is the one person in your life that you can share anything with and will hold you accountable in the areas where you are committed to growing? Are you currently walking "in the light" (transparently) with this person?

3. Since you have been reading this book, what is one other Bible verse we have explored that you feel should be committed to your memory? Write it below:

CHAPTER 9

Inside-Out Stewardship

We are going to shift modes as we conclude this section on the second CORE discipline, offering God everything. In the last chapter, we dug a little deeper, outlining five ways we can walk in freedom so that nothing holds us back from offering God everything in our lives. But in this chapter, I want to get even more practical because when it comes to offering ourselves to God, we simply cannot skip the topic of what is known as Biblical stewardship.

> *A steward is someone who faithfully and diligently takes care of something that belongs to someone else. They also use what has been entrusted to them for its intended purpose.*

That definition alone is worth rereading....slowly!

As Christians, we are to faithfully steward everything God has given us. But here is the big idea of this chapter:

Everything we have, including our very own life, is not our own!

This fundamental truth of the Christian faith is based on 1 Corinthians 6:19-20. This verse tells us that the Holy Spirit, the one who helps us to live out our faith from the inside out, lives within our very bodies as His temple.

"Do you not know that your body is a temple for the Holy Spirit, who is in you, whom you have received from God. You are not your own; you were bought at a price. Therefore, honor God with your body."

When we received Christ at our point of salvation, a transfer of ownership took place. Every aspect of our lives, including our very bodies, became His when we invited Jesus to become Lord of our lives. We are not our own and our lives do not belong to us any longer. We are now stewarding our lives as though they belong to God. Much of our lives boil down to three main areas that I want to encourage you to steward faithfully—our time, our talents, and our treasure.

Stewarding Our Time

One of the most precious things we have in this life is our time. Statistically speaking, a simple google search reveals:

- The average lifespan for men is 84.3 years.

- The average lifespan for women is 86.6 years.

The question is: Am I using my time wisely for his glory? I love Psalms 90:12,

"Teach us to number our days, that we may gain a heart of wisdom."

In other words, "God, help me to steward the time you've given me to the best of my ability." Solomon, whom the Bible calls the wisest man to ever live, concluded this about much of life in Ecclesiastes 1:2,

"Meaningless! Meaningless!" says the Teacher. "Utterly meaningless! Everything is meaningless."

Solomon was coming to the end of his days and concluded something about the nature of life. We must make up our minds as to what is meaningless and what is meaningful in our life. Therefore, I want to encourage you to take inventory of the use of your time in four key categories. It's an acronym that I call The Four T.I.M.E Zones Of Life:

Four T.I.M.E Zones Of Life

- **T**ime with God. Is spending time with God a priority in my life? Do I value growing in my awareness of His presence in my life?

- **I**ntimacy with others. Am I investing the right kind of time into the most important relationships of my life—namely my family, my close friends, and the people I am trying to reach? Do I value Biblical fellowship, doing life with others, and dare I say.... having a little fun in life?

- **M**inistry involvement in my church, workplace, and community. Am I a ministry minded individual? Do I regularly attend church but also invest my time serving others? Do I strive to add value to those I work with and to those I live next to in my neighborhood?

- **E**xcellence in the workplace and at home. Do I work hard, and do I work intentionally? Do I do everything to the glory of God at home and at work? Do I strive to be the very best employee or stay at home parent I possibly can be? Do I treat my time at work as worship and a means to witness to the unreached?

Our time on this earth is short, relatively speaking, and we would do well to take inventory as to how we are stewarding our time.

Stewarding our Talents

Releasing our ministry is the topic of the next section of this book, but there is something pivotal we need to understand now. If we don't belong to ourselves, then certainly our gifts, abilities, and talents don't belong to us either. They belong to God. Therefore, our gifts should be used for His glory and not our own. There is no place for pride as we fulfill our God given purposes. If we can settle this truth deep in our hearts now, then we can move forward in releasing our talents to a greater level of impact for the glory of God, and not the glory of ourselves. But more on this soon!

Stewarding our Treasure

Ok, this last one is big because it has to do with our money. Oh, wait a minute. I said *our* money, didn't I? Sorry about that. It's just easy to forget that everything we are and everything we have belongs to God. If we belong to God, then so does *our* money. In fact, that means we are called to channel financial resources responsibly to take care of our lives and to fund ministry to others within the local church and beyond.

In the Old Testament, God's people, called the Israelites, were required by law to tithe. The word tithe means "a tenth part." The Israelites were to return 10% of everything they earned back to the Lord–whether it be livestock, produce from the land, or their monetary income. This currency was to be used for the care of the temple, to take care of the priests, and to meet the needs of the people.

God took the tithe very seriously, so seriously in fact that he invited the people to do something that He would never do again in any other place within Scripture. He challenged them to test Him. They were to honor Him with the principle of the tithe, and He would honor this principle with incredible promises. Look at what God says about the tithe, the test, and the promise He would fulfill for His people when they met their obligation in Malachi 3:10,

> "Bring the whole tithe into the storehouse, that there may be
> food in my house. Test me in this, says the Lord Almighty, and see
> if I will not throw open the floodgates of heaven and pour out
> so much blessing that you will not have room enough for it."

God told the people that if they would honor Him with just a tenth, then He would pour out His blessings upon them in abundance. But He also stated that failure to do so was the equivalent of robbing Him of what was rightfully His anyways. Not only that, but failure to tithe would also result in God's people robbing themselves of the blessings that would otherwise follow their obedience.

Some say that tithing is no longer a New Testament principle. But I love what Jesus said about the tithe in the book of Matthew. He was confronting a group of people called the Pharisees who were known to exercise their religious duty but without heartfelt devotion. Listen to what Jesus said to them in Matthew 23:

> Matthew 23:23 "Woe to you, teachers of the law and Pharisees, you hypocrites! You give a tenth of your spices—mint, dill and cumin. But you have neglected the more important matters of the law—justice, mercy and faithfulness. You should have practiced the latter, without neglecting the former."

Jesus outright said that they (and we) should have practiced the latter (tithing). But he then pivoted to what was really at stake with their giving, and with our giving for that matter—the heart. Here is something worth remembering:

> *What comes from our hand as an offering is in direct relationship to the condition of our heart.*

And this is never truer than when it comes to our...uh...God's money. Consider the following when it comes to the heart of giving:

Our giving reveals our treasure.

Matthew 6:19-21 says,

> "Do not store up for yourselves treasures on earth, where moths and vermin destroy, and where thieves break in and steal. But store up for yourselves treasures in heaven, where moths and vermin do not destroy, and where thieves do not break in and steal. For where your treasure is, there your heart will be also."

Jesus said plainly in this passage that we are to store up treasures in heaven, meaning that we should invest into the things of this life that are eternal and not temporal. Investing into people, by giving to a local church whose mission is to reach the lost and disciple the found, is the absolute best thing we can invest into this side of heaven. The truth is, we put our (God's) money into the things we treasure the most. And when we treasure what God treasures, we will give with a joyful and grateful attitude. 2 Corinthians 9:7 says,

> "For God loves a cheerful giver."

We give cheerfully when we treasure what God treasures!

Our giving reveals our take on life.

Look at what Jesus then says about our stewardship from Matthew 6:22-23

> "The eye is the lamp of the body. If your eyes are healthy, your whole body will be full of light. But if your eyes are unhealthy, your whole body will be full of darkness. If then the light within you is darkness, how great is that darkness! "No one can serve two masters. Either you will hate the one and love the other, or you will be devoted to the one and despise the other. You cannot serve both God and money."

Boy, there is a lot in these few verses. It ends with a sober warning about serving two masters and the impossibility of bowing down to both God and money. But did you catch what Jesus said about the eyes? He said that if a person's eyes are good, their whole body will be full of light. But if they are bad, a person's whole life would be filled with darkness. What did He mean by this?

Remember, the New Testament was written in mostly Greek, and the purest form of the Greek word for eye in this passage is "generous." And the Greek word for "bad eye" is "stingy eye." Whoa. Connect the dots with me now and read the passage again:

If a man's eyes are generous, his whole body will be full of light. If a man's eyes are stingy, his whole body will be full of darkness.

Jesus is saying that the key to a wholesome and fulfilling life is to have a generous eye toward others! I love that and I want to be a believer with a generous eye, not a stingy one. To have a generous eye towards others means to desire to use what God has given us to bless and enrich someone else in any possible way. This means looking for ways to verbally affirm and encourage others. This means seeking out ways to serve the people we live with and work next to every day. This also means having a generous eye with our financial resources. It ultimately means to embrace the truth that there is nothing more fulfilling than blessing others! As I've heard it said, "To live is to give" and I absolutely believe this to be true!

Our giving reveals our trust.

Keep reading through Matthew 6 and you will also notice once again, just as we explored from Malachi 3, a promise connected to a divine principle. The promise is simply that God will provide for us. Perhaps you should read these verses out loud from Matthew 6:25-27:

"Therefore I tell you, do not worry about your life, what you will eat or drink; or about your body, what you will wear. Is not life more than food, and the body more than clothes? Look at the birds of the air; they do not sow or reap or store away in barns, and yet your heavenly Father feeds them. Are you not much more valuable than they? Can any one of you by worrying add a single hour to your life?"

And listen to what Paul declares to the Philippians, a group of people who helped provide financial and material resources to take care of him and advance his ministry in Philippians 4:19:

"And my God will meet all your needs according to his glorious riches in Christ Jesus."

When we are stewarding God's resources Biblically, we can find true rest in the reality that God takes care of us as His children. He will indeed supply all of our needs according to His riches and glory. And as a result, we can embrace what Jesus said in Matthew 6, "Do not worry!" Here's one last bottom line truth:

God's wisdom will always prevail over our worry.

When we apply God's word to any area of our life, including the finances He has entrusted to us, we will see His Word at work in our life. We will truly see His provision if we obey the principle of the tithe and trust His promise.

Conclusion

We are called to be stewards—believers who recognize that we own nothing and are called to channel the resources of heaven entrusted to us in such a way to bring glory to God and advance His kingdom. Exploring the way in which we steward our time, our talent, and our treasure is a great starting point to evaluating how we are doing in this vital discipline of the Christian faith. Let's steward well, with a generous eye toward others and with a heart to honor God in every domain of life.

Week 9 Workout

- Consider the challenge to start tithing if you are not already doing so. Appendix 3 of this book is a starter budget you can fill out that includes tithing. What areas of your budget do you need to trim or cut out to remain faithful with the tithe? Now, would you be willing to embark on a 90 Day Tithe Challenge? Every week, reconcile your budget, keep track of your expenses, and be faithful to tithe no matter what. Give yourself the time to be diligent in this area and to see the Word of God begin to take root and work in your life. And let your pastor know about your decision, so that he/she can be in prayer for you during this three- month window as you embrace this discipline!

- Continue with the book of John by reading chapters 16-18 and doing an IRA from one of the chapters. Practice praying using the PRAY acronym.

- Read the next chapter in this book.

Reflection Questions For Individual Or Small Group Use

1. Look back through the four zones in regard to stewarding our time. Which zone is your strongest? Which is your weakest? Why?

2. Do you feel as though you struggle with pride when it comes to the gifts and abilities God has given you? What are some things we can remember in order to keep our hearts humble?

3. And finally, how does this chapter resonate with you in regard to money? What struggles do you have in keeping track of your own budget? What questions or fears do you have when it comes to tithing? Do you tithe?

SECTION 4

Welcome to section 3 of our spiritual workout together! The name of this book is Inside Out—Building the CORE of Your Christian Faith.

So far, we have explored two spiritual disciplines that would fall more into the category of "Inside" when it comes "Inside Out."

- Connecting with God and

- Offering God our everything

In this section, however, we are pivoting to the two disciplines that comprise the "Out" of "Inside Out." They are:

- Releasing our ministry

- Engaging in outreach and missions

This section is all about releasing our ministry. But before you make the statement "But I'm not called to full time ministry," please understand the premise of this section. This section is for everyone who is a Christ follower, not just those called to full time ministry. The reason is because the Bible is clear that God has called all of us to minister to others. In fact, Ephesians 4:11-12 makes it clear that the purpose of pastors is to actually equip laypeople for acts of ministry and service. We are all called to use what the Lord has given us to add value to others, serve them, and to ultimately build them into mature disciples of Jesus Christ. God wants to use us all—yes even you—to minister to others!

But many believers haven't yet discovered their God-given gifts or have allowed them to become dormant. These gifts need to be stirred and released again through their lives. Still others are wrestling through a sense that "there must be more" and are looking for a way to take their gifts to the next level.

If any of these scenarios speak to you, look at what we will be discussing:

- Chapter 10–Inside-Out Purpose (The four platforms God uses to reveal His will and purposes for our lives).

- Chapter 11–Inside-Out Giftedness (A closer look at our spiritual gifts).

- Chapter 12–Inside-Out Release (Releasing our ministry in the face of the devil's resistance).

My prayer for you at this point in this discipleship journey is that you are sensing spiritual momentum like never before. Keep reading the chapters of this book. Keep watching the videos that are posted online. Keep reading your Bible and praying daily. And keep meeting with the accountability partner you have selected to join you in this journey.

Keep on keeping on, and let's look at releasing a greater level of ministry from our lives!

CHAPTER 10

Inside-Out Purpose

I was a junior in high school and belonged to an organization on my campus that mentored younger students. We visited freshman classes and presented sessions on topics such as overcoming peer pressure, dating, and the many other hot topics teenagers still face today. I finished my part of the presentation and still remember what I thought when I handed the microphone off to the next person, "I think I have potential when it comes to public speaking." I didn't know at the time I would become a preacher. I just knew that I felt like I had just tapped into a gift that God deposited into my life that I didn't even know existed. I simply put myself out there to do something I had never done, and that one courageous step contributed to a lifetime calling.

That first public speaking opportunity was like the discovery of buried treasure. And that is exactly what it is like whenever we discover the talents, abilities, and gifts God has given us and start using them for His glory.

I am not sure what your God-given gifts and talents are. They certainly do not have to be related to public speaking at all. They can be working with your hands, opening your home to others, loving on children, being a natural encourager, leading others to accomplish tasks, organizing things, or providing for others through generosity. They can be public or private. They can be center stage or behind the scenes. But one thing is absolutely certain.

If God is at work *in* your life, He desires to be at work *through* your life!

We must look again at our CORE verse, Philippians 2:12-13, paying close attention to the last five words.

"Therefore, my dear friends, as you have always obeyed—not only in my presence, but now much more in my absence—continue to work out your salvation with fear and trembling, for it is God who works in you *to will and to act according to his good purpose"* (italics added).

The punchline of this verse, and this entire book for that matter, is that we are called to live out the very purposes that God is working in us. These purposes are both general and specific. They include the purposes God has for every believer such as fulfilling the Great Commission and living life in a manner that brings glory and honor to His name. But they also include His specific purposes for our lives individually. I love Ephesians 2:10,

"For we are God's workmanship, created in Christ Jesus to do good works, which God prepared in advance for us to do."

God, since the beginning of time, has prepared good works and well thought out plans for all of us to do and accomplish. And God works on the inside of us so that we may walk and flesh out those good works He has prepared for our lives. That is spiritual synergy in its purest form—walking out what God is working within! This chapter highlights the four platforms God uses to help us discover our purposes and achieve a greater level of this synergy in our lives.

(Note: This chapter is designed to be interactive. So, grab a pen and answer the questions after each subsection. Allow the Holy Spirit to speak to you through this process of discovery!)

Platform #1–I discover my purpose through my PASSIONS.

What do you love to do and what are you good at? I heard this same question asked this way once, "What is your woe point?" Paul said in 1 Corinthians 9:16 "Woe to me if I do not preach the gospel!" Paul was essentially saying, "If I don't do anything else in life, I must preach the gospel. In fact, woe to me if I do not! My life is incomplete, unfulfilling, and downright dissatisfying unless I preach the gospel."

So, what is your woe point? What are a few things you must do in order to feel fulfilled in life? Start by answering the question, "If you had to choose just one or two things to do in order to feel like you were living life to the fullest, what would they be?" For me, public speaking is one of them. I also love to write. And still another one is leading people to fulfill a vision. If I'm not doing these things, my emotions feel like "woe to me" and I feel very unfulfilled.

So, let me ask you: What do you like to do? What are you good at? And what is your woe point?

1. I'm good at _____

2. I like to_____

3. One of my woe points would be_____

Platform #2–I discover my purpose through my PAST and specific POINTS OF PAIN.

Your past, when surrendered to the Lord and filtered through the redemptive work of Jesus Christ, can become a life message to others. For me, I grew up in an atmosphere often marked by depression. One of my life messages to others is that true joy is based on the presence of God on the inside of us and not the changing circumstances of the world all around us. Another life message is that if God can give me–someone once deeply plagued by insecurity–significance and meaning, then He can do the same for anyone! A third one would simply be that God has called us to live as victors and not victims and He knows how to get us from where we are to where we long to be.

One way to start discovering God's purpose for your life is by exploring potential life messages God has written for you as a result of turning your past over to Him. Ask yourself, "What themes and character traits of God always seem to surface in my life? What does God always seem to be teaching me about Himself?" And finally, "if I had to tell everyone in the world just one thing I have learned about God, what would it be?" Answer these questions and determine what purposes of God are in your life today as a result of how He has helped you deal with your past.

What is one character trait you have learned about God? What does God always seem to be teaching you about Himself?

_____

What is a life message you would shout out to others as a result of dealing with your past?

_____

—

What is one thing you have been through in your past that God could use to help someone else today?

_____

Now, after having a heart to heart with yourself, read what Paul says in 2 Corinthians 1:3-5.

"Praise be to the God and Father of our Lord Jesus Christ, the Father of compassion and the God of all comfort, who comforts us in all our troubles, so that we can comfort those in any trouble with the comfort we ourselves receive from God. For just as we share abundantly in the sufferings of Christ, so also our comfort abounds through Christ."

One result of allowing God to help us deal with our past is that we gain the increased capacity to release the compassion we have received from God to others. This is how our ministry becomes branded with true authenticity that greatly influences people. As a result, people actually receive what we release from our lives because it is flowing from a place of genuine humility and heartfelt concern for others.

Platform #3–I discover my purpose through divinely revealed PURPOSES and PROMISES from God.

I just gave you two different platforms we can explore to discover God's purposes for our lives. But this next one is perhaps the most important, because it has everything to do with simply hearing God speak to you. A question I often hear as a pastor is, "how do I know when God is speaking to me?" Let me give you a brief crash course on hearing God's voice. Here are five ways we hear God's voice:

- Through His Word

The primary way God speaks to us and reveals His will for our lives is through His Word. Reading the Bible is a sure-fire way to have confidence that we are hearing from God. For when we open His word, God opens His mouth to speak to us. Every other way in which He speaks will always be in line with His Word and will never contradict it. I encourage you to pour yourself into His Word and you will see that God will use it to pour His will into you. Spending time in God's Word opens the door for Him to speak to you in other ways as well.

- Through prayer

Another way God speaks to us is by placing thoughts into our minds as we pray. 1 Corinthians 2:9-10 says, "However, as it is written: "No eye has seen, no ear has heard, no mind has conceived what God has prepared for those who love him—but God has *revealed it to us by his spirit*" (italics added). God reveals His plans for us as we set our minds on Him through prayer. People often say they know when God is speaking to them because they feel impressed in their spirit about something. This impression is a divine knowing from God that early church fathers used to call "the growing knowing." And this wonderful growing knowing of God's plan for your life is cultivated through the discipline of prayer and spending time in His presence.

- Through others

God also speaks to us through other people we trust such as account-ability partners, friends who are also growing in their faith, pastors, or other spiritual leaders. I'll never forget my high school English teacher looking at me and saying, "I really believe you'll make a good writer one day." Those words have stuck with me to this day and I believe it was God speaking to me through someone else's encouragement. Other times I have received counsel through my pastor whose words often line up with what I am already sensing in my spirit about something. Sometimes another person's advice is the catalyst I need to get my spirit in tune with God's Spirit about a decision at hand. The bottom line is that God speaks to us through others.

- Through the peace of the Holy Spirit

Galatians 5:16 commands us to "walk after the Spirit." That essentially means that we walk closely with the Lord in obedience. I have noticed that when I walk in close fellowship with the Holy Spirit, my spiritual radar becomes sensitive and I can more easily discern how His presence is leading and guiding me. This is often called "the release and restraint of the Spirit." As I walk to please Him, he restrains and releases me in regards to matters of obedience and matters of His will for my life. In this way, the Holy Spirit serves as an internal compass that bears witness to the will of God for us. By the Spirit, we can sense the "yes" or "no" of God with the decisions we need to make. The "yes" of God will produce a peace in our Spirits. But the "no" or "not now" of the Holy Spirit will often cause an unsettled feeling within us. A good rule of thumb is to follow peace and stop or slow down if you sense anything different!

- Through visions and dreams

This one can be dangerous and, quite frankly, abused if we are not care-ful. However, if a believer is a person of the Word who prays regularly, is in touch with the Spirit of God, and is walking under the authority of spir-itual leadership, then I absolutely believe God will speak to them also through visions and dreams. The reason I write books today is because this is exactly what happened to me when I was 18 years old. Night after night I would lay in my bed, listening to praise and worship, and see myself typing at a computer. I was spending consistent time in the Word of God during the day and as I worshipped Him at night, He divinely revealed part of His plan for my life. And I believe He can do the same for you.

Having said all that, what has God revealed to you about your life up to this point? What promises do you feel like God has whispered into your heart by the Holy Spirit? Remember, the same Holy Spirit who works in you to will and to act according to His good purpose also reveals the mind of God and His mission for your life. God longs to speak His purposes and His promises to those who have inclined their hearts to Him and are willing to listen!

What are some divine purposes/promises you feel like God has given you?

_____

_____

_____

_____

_____

Which of the five ways in which we hear God's voice are strong for you? Weak?

_____

_____

_____

_____

_____

What is your starting point to fulfilling these purposes OR taking them to another level? Who is one person you can share this with? Have you shared them with your pastor yet? Why or why not?

_____

_____

_____

_____

_____

Platform #4—I discover my purpose through my PERSONALITY.
Ok, enough deep stuff for a moment. Let's talk briefly about our personality because our personality is one sure way, we can discover who God has created us to be. By understanding our personality, we can then realize some of the potential that lies within the borders of who we naturally are. There is a condensed version of the DISC personality profile in appendix 4 of this book. Turn there and complete the short profile now!

What is your personality based on the DISC assessment?

_____

_____

How do you see your personality meshing with your purposes? How do the two go hand in hand?

_____

_____

_____

_____

_____

Conclusion

This chapter was about the discovery of God's purposes and the four platforms God often uses to reveal them to us. Our passions, our past, our divinely revealed purposes, and our personality are all just starting points to discovering all that God has for us. In the next chapter, we will take one last spiritual gifts test and tie everything together in such a way to give you a good starting point as to what is next for you in regards to being used by God. Keep reading, keep working through the exercises, and continue to read your Bible. If you have made it this far in the journey, you are hopefully experiencing tremendous growth in your walk with the Lord.

Week 10 Spiritual Workout

- Completing the interactive exercises in this chapter will serve as your spiritual workout for this week. However, I would highly encourage you to get together with one other person and share your insights with them. Allow them to speak into your answers. I have found that people closest to me, like my wife, can be a huge asset in sifting through deep questions like "who am I?", "what things am I good at?", and "what is God calling me to do?"

- Finish the book of John this week (chapters 19-21) and do another IRA. Practice praying using the PRAY acronym.

- Read the next chapter in this book!

Reflection Questions

1. Which of the four platforms does God seem to use the most to speak to you? Are there any other ways not mentioned in this chapter that God uses to reveal His will for your life?

2. For example, another way God reveals His will for our lives is through natural circumstances. When was there a season in your life that God seemed to speak to you through open and closed doors?

3. Share your personality profile with a friend or small group. Do the people closest to you agree with the results of your profile? What do they add to your conclusions?

CHAPTER 11

Inside-Out Giftedness

Let me start off this chapter with a bold statement I believe you will agree with:

There is nothing, I repeat NOTHING, like being used by God!

There is nothing like the feeling of walking in your God-given gifts, abilities, and talents.

In the last chapter, we looked at four broad ways in which we can discover God's purposes and plans for our lives. In this chapter, we are going to put the cherry on top by taking a spiritual gifts survey. We will then take a closer look at the Biblical backdrop behind the gifts given to us by the Holy Spirit and found in the Word of God.

Look at two passages of Scripture that speak about the gifts:

- 1 Corinthians 12:4-11 There are different kinds of gifts, but the same Spirit. There are different kinds of service, but the same Lord. There are different kinds of working, but the same God works all of them in all men. Now to each one the manifestation of the Spirit is given for the common good. To one there is given through the Spirit the message of wisdom, to another the message of knowledge by means of the same Spirit, to another faith by the same Spirit, to another gifts of healing by that one Spirit, to another miraculous powers, to another prophecy, to another distinguishing between spirits, to another speaking in different kinds of tongues, and to still another the interpretation of tongues. All these are the work of one and the same Spirit, and he gives them to each one, just as he determines.

- Romans 12:6-8 We have different gifts, according to the grace given to each of us. If your gift is prophesying, then let him use it in proportion to his faith. If it is serving, let him serve; if it is teaching, let him teach; if it is encouraging, let him encourage; if it is contributing to the needs of others, let him give generously; if it is leadership, let him govern diligently; if it is showing mercy, let him do it cheerfully.

The gifts are usually broken down into two broad categories: spiritual and ministry. The spiritual gifts, such as those found in 1 Corinthians 12:1-11, are exactly what they sound like. They are spiritual in nature and function to build and encourage someone's faith. Words of wisdom and knowledge fall into this category. The ministry gifts like the ones mentioned in Romans 12 are usually more pragmatic in nature. They usually translate into some kind of area of service within a local church and minister to both the spiritual and practical needs of others. For example, the gifts of leadership, generosity, and hospitality would fit into this category. It is important to note that every believer has at least one gift but can also be used in multiple gifts as well.

Having said all that, let's take a spiritual gifts survey!

The spiritual gifts survey is found in appendix 5 in the back of this book. Turn there now and take the test. (Note: The number one rule of thumb when taking any spiritual gifts test is to simply write down the first answer or response that comes to mind. Don't think too hard on it. Just answer the questions and move through the survey!)

(Dramatic pause inserted at this point while you take the test.......)

Welcome back! Now write out your spiritual gifts from the test below:

_____

_____

_____

_____

_____

In just a minute, we are going to tie together the discovery process from the last chapter and this chapter. But before we do that, I really want us all to understand four quick things about spiritual gifts.

Our gifts and the life of the Holy Spirit within us go hand in hand
Spiritual gifts have also been called spiritual graces or grace gifts. This is simply because any gift of God at work *through* our lives is only made possible by the grace of God at work *in* our lives. Look again at what Paul says in 1 Corinthians 12:4-7 and notice the role of the Holy Spirit,

"There are different kinds of gifts, but the same Spirit. There are different kinds of service, but the same Lord. There are different kinds of working, but the same God works all of them in all men. Now to each one the manifestation of the Spirit is given for the common good."

Look at what he says further in verse 11 of the same chapter,

"All these are the work of one and the same Spirit, and he distributes them to each one, just as he determines."

Clearly, the spiritual gifts in our lives are deposited in us, developed within us, and deployed through us by the Holy Spirit. Again, remember Philippians 2:12-13. The Holy Spirit is at work *in* us to be at work *through* us. Therefore, the punchline of this entire chapter could be summed up as this: If we want to be used by God, we need to stay close to the Holy Spirit. We cultivate our communion with Him through the Word, prayer, and obedience. And the greater our communion with Him, the greater our calling is released through our lives to minister to others. And by calling, I simply mean using our gifts and abilities to bless others and glorify the Lord.

Our gifts and our legacy go hand in hand

One of the most popular verses in all of the Bible is Matthew 25:21, "Well done my good and faithful servant." Most of us think this is the verse Jesus will speak to us when we enter into the courts of heaven. However, it is found in the parable of the buried talents. Jesus' point is clear. Those who will hear "well done" will be those who put to work the gifts and abilities He has given them to bless others and advance the kingdom of God while on this earth. This is the greatest legacy we can leave behind. It is the legacy of leaving no gift buried in the sands of time but rather allowing God to fully use us as He sees fit. Jesus said in John 15:16, "You did not choose me, but I chose you and appointed you so that you might go and bear fruit—fruit that will last." The goal of the Holy Spirit in our hearts is to produce lasting fruit in both our character and our calling while on this earth. And it will be these two things for which we become known and remembered and will ultimately determine the kind of legacy we leave behind.

Our gifts and love go hand in hand

Have you ever heard the song, "What's love got to do with it?" In the case of spiritual gifts, everything! Being used by God without the love of God burning in our hearts for others is dangerous. Without love, our gifts can be abused and used for selfish gain at the expense of others. Without God's love, our gifts can puff up our hearts to unprecedented levels of pride and arrogance. Paul said it this way in 1 Corinthians 13:1-3,

> If I speak in the tongues of men or of angels, but do not have love, I am only a resounding gong or a clanging cymbal. 2 If I have the gift of prophecy and can fathom all mysteries and all knowledge, and if I have a faith that can move mountains, but do not have love, I am nothing. 3 If I give all I possess to the poor and give over my body to hardship that I may boast, but do not have love, I gain nothing.

If love is not the motive of our hearts as we desire to be used more in the gifts God has given us, we reduce ourselves to sounding like clanging cymbals. Our motive becomes getting attention for ourselves rather than blessing others and drawing attention to God. Our goal must be to love others through our gifts, and we must keep this motive before us as we learn to step out in faith in what God has given us.

Spiritual gifts must be developed just as any other life skill

The Scripture tells us to eagerly desire the spiritual gifts (1 Corinthians 14:1). Desire is the first step in being used by God. The cry of our hearts must be, "God use me however you see fit!".

Desire is the first step, but development is a close second. I hate to sound trivial when saying this but being used in the gifts God has given us takes practice. Whether it's learning to hear the voice of God on behalf of others in order to encourage them or leading a Bible study, our gifts are developed over time as we put them into practice and grow in them. The important thing is to discover them and get started!

Conclusion

Now, let's put the last two chapters together by answering the following five questions. This will serve as your weekly workout exercise. But before you do so, let me warn you about something. The chief enemy of your life, the devil himself, does not like it when you get serious about serving the Lord through your gifts. In fact, I tell people all the time that when you start taking steps to be used by God, the devil will take a step toward you. In fact, his whole goal is to try and restrain you from being released into greater levels of kingdom influence. Therefore, in the next and final chapter of this section, we are going to further explore the idea of God's character to release us and the devil's character to restrain us. It's release vs. restrain, and it is a battle that God has equipped us to win. So, keep reading! I want to make sure you understand his four playgrounds and the weapons you have to defeat him on his own turf!

Week 11 Spiritual Workout—Fill out the worksheet below and let's put it all together:

From the last chapter, write out your top passions, interests, and hobbies here:

_____

_____

_____

From the last chapter, write out in 3 sentences how you feel like God can use your past and the points of pain that came along with it to bless and encourage others:

_____

_____

_____

What is your personality based on the DISC survey you took last chapter?

_____

_____

_____

What are your top three spiritual gifts based on the inventory that you just took?

_____

_____

_____

What ministry or outreach at your church do you see as the best fit in which to serve based on the questions you have just answered? You may need to have a conversation with your pastor now about how to best utilize your gifts!

_____

_____

- Secondly, for your Bible reading this week, read Genesis 1-3 and do one IRA. This will give you a good framework for the next chapter in this book. Practice praying using the PRAY acronym.

- Read the next chapter in this book.

Reflection Questions For Individual Or Small Group Use

1. Share the results of your spiritual gifts test with a friend or a small group. How did they respond to the results of your test? Did they validate and confirm the results based on how well they know you?

2. What are some of the dangers of being used in our gifts without God's love anchoring our hearts as we release our ministry? A better way to ask this question may be: What happens in a believer's life when they are operating in their gifts without love?

3. Describe someone you know who really seems to operate in the gifts God has given them. What traits characterize their life? What could you glean from that person?

CHAPTER 12

Inside-Out Release

One of my favorite verses in all of the Bible is Isaiah 61:1-2 because it describes the character and nature of Jesus' work while He was on this earth. It also describes the nature of His ministry that He desires to continue in the earth today through the power of the Holy Spirit in our lives. Look at the word that I have italicized in this passage:

> Isaiah 61:1-2 The Spirit of the Sovereign Lord is on me, because the Lord has anointed me to preach good news to the poor. He has sent me to bind up the broken-hearted, to proclaim freedom for the captives and release from darkness for the prisoners, to proclaim the year of the Lord's favor.

The word release here means to free from condemnation and confinement. This freedom, this release, is the very thing Jesus Christ came to do. He came to release us from a spiritual prison into a fulfilled and abundant life. Read John 10:10,

> The thief comes only to steal and kill and destroy; I have come that they may have life and have it to the full.

Did you catch the first part of this verse? You and I have an enemy of our soul named the devil. And while it is God's will to release us, it is the devil's will to restrain us. To restrain means to hold back, repress, and keep control over. One work of the devil is to limit us and to reduce the amount of effective ministry that flows through us to others. He ultimately wants to confine us to lower levels of living which is in stark contrast to the abundant life Jesus came to give us.

Let's explore who exactly this "devil" is and how we can walk in greater levels of authority over him so that we can release effective ministry to others.

Who exactly is "the enemy?"

His name is the devil, Satan, or Lucifer. He is described as a thief, the one who tempts us, and the Father of all lies. As we just looked at, his ultimate purpose and his primary agenda behind all that he says and does is to steal, kill, and destroy. The Lord Jesus Himself is the author of life, Satan is the author of death. Jesus is full of light; Satan is full of darkness. Jesus is the purest form of love that mankind has craved since the creation of the world. Satan is the highest expression of hatred and evil mankind has ever known.

Satan is the antithesis of all that God embodies. But it wasn't always that way. The Bible makes it clear that Lucifer used to hold a prominent position in heaven as an angel. But something took place in his heart that led to his downfall. Satan became jealous of the glory being ascribed to Jesus and wanted that same glory for himself. The concept of pride originated with the devil, and it was this pride and deep-seated arrogance that caused him to lose his place before Jesus in heaven. God the Father banished him from heaven and cast him, along with about 1/3 of the angels in heaven, down to this earth as judgement. This host of fallen angels, along with the devil, now comprise the spiritual forces of evil at work in the world and in the heavenly realms as described in Ephesians 6.

Satan's sole purpose, along with this new kingdom of darkness, was to get back at God and rob God of the glory due His name. His primary means to do this was by attacking God's creation. After all, he himself had fallen, and the only way to get even with God was to cause

His beloved creation to fall as well. And this is exactly what he did in the garden of Eden. I challenge you to put this book down and read the first three chapters of the Bible, Genesis 1-3. It will help you to understand the nature of the fall and the nature of our foe behind it.

Fast forward to Genesis 3:15. This is God pronouncing judgement against the devil for his part in the fall of man. He says,

> "*he* will crush your head, and you will strike his heel." (Italics added)

The "he" in this verse is speaking of Jesus and God says that Jesus will ultimately crush the head of the devil. Think about it, the first mention of the victory we now have through faith in Jesus was declared by God in just the third chapter of the entire Bible. Several thousand years later, this victory took place through the death, burial, and resurrection of Jesus Christ. I love Colossians 2:15,

> "And having disarmed the powers and authorities, he made a public spectacle of them, triumphing over them by the cross."

And now Jesus' victory has become my victory over sin and Satan. In fact, I would highly encourage you to spend some time reading Romans 6-8. It's an incredible discourse written by Paul that outlines what it means to walk in the Spirit and live victoriously. He concludes with one of the most famous passages in all of Scripture, Romans 8:37

> "No, in all these things we are more than conquerors through him who loved us."

The devil is defeated, and we are more than conquerors. But we must learn to appropriate this victory in our lives and resist the devil and his schemes. James 4:7 says,

> "Submit yourselves, then, to God. Resist the devil, and he will flee from you."

Let's look at four ways to submit to God and resist the devil so that we can live our lives in victory and release ministry to others as a result. As we do so, I am also going to highlight the four playgrounds of the enemy.

1. Discern the "DGRS" of the devil.

The fall of mankind started with a simple question consisting of four words whispered by the devil into the heart of Adam and Eve. "Did God Really Say?" I call this the DGRS of the devil. It was through this question that the devil planted seeds of doubt in Eve's mind regarding the goodness of God. At first, she answered correctly. "God did say," she responded. But the devil is very persistent. He wore her down and weakened her with the same question over and over again, the same way he does with us. And the more Eve entertained the question, the more those seeds of doubt within her grew. And it was her doubt that eventually led to her downfall and ultimately the downfall of man.

The devil is still asking variations of this same question to us today. Some variations could be:

- "Did God really say that you are forgiven?"

- "Did God really say that He loves you and has a plan for your life?"

- "Did God really say that you are not alone and that He will never leave you or forsake you?

We must learn to discern when the enemy is trying to cast doubt into our minds concerning the character and nature of God. We must learn to spot the "DGRS" of the enemy. We must then answer the doubt with the "GDS".... the "God Did Say," of the Bible:

- "God did say that I am forgiven and free from condemnation and therefore guilt" (Romans 8:1, 1 John 1:9).

- "God did say that He loves me with an everlasting love and Has a plan for my life" (Jeremiah 29:11, Jeremiah 31:3).

- "God did say that He will be with me always and will never leave me nor forsake me" (Joshua 1:5, Matthew 28:20).

Read through Matthew 4:1-11 and you will read how Satan attacked Jesus and how Jesus overcame him by declaring the "GDS" of God! After a series of exchanges with the devil, Jesus finally said, "Away from me Satan!" We too must get to that point as we resist the doubt of the enemy. I don't ever want to sound like I am trivializing spiritual warfare issues but eventually we must declare, "Talk to the hand because the heart isn't gonna hear it!" We have to get to the point where we simply refuse to allow what the devil is whispering in our heads to sink into our hearts.

When you find yourself doubting anything about God or what He says to you, declare the "God Did Say" over and over again. And you will find that as you stand your ground against doubt, and allow God's word to penetrate your unbelief, something powerful will transpire. You will find that the very things you once doubted the most will be the things you declare the most to others. God will transform your doubt into rock solid faith that He will then use to release others from their own unbelief!

Summary: Playground number #1 of the devil is doubt. Doubt is usually anchored in some form of a "DGRS" of the enemy. You overcome the doubt by declaring the "GDS" of God.

2. Learn to spot the not.
John 8:44 tells us something insightful into the character of the enemy.

John 8:44 He was a murderer from the beginning, not holding to the truth, for there is no truth in him. When he lies, he speaks his native language, for he is a liar and the father of lies.

When you go back to Genesis 3 you not only see the devil asking Adam and Eve "Did God Really Say?" but you then see him telling them a bold face lie that directly contradicted the Word of God. "You will surely not die," he said. (Genesis 3:4) God outright told Adam and Eve that death would be the consequence should they disobey Him. And the enemy, after casting a little doubt, was then able to insert an outright lie into their minds.

A little doubt can lead to a lot of deception in our lives as well. However, John 8:32 says,

"then you will know the truth, and the truth will set you free."

When we pour our hearts into God's Word, we discover and grow in our knowledge of the truth. And when we know the truth, it becomes much easier to discern and defeat the lies of the enemy. I am reminded of an illustration one of my mentors shared with me when I first got saved. He told me that in the early years of the U.S. Treasury, the government had a unique way of training employees to recognize counterfeit money. He said they would train their workers to spot counterfeit bills by making the employees look at thousands of real bills that would cross their eyes on a conveyor belt in front of them. Occasionally they would slip in a counterfeit. Because the workers' eyes were so trained to see the real thing, they could easily spot the counterfeit. The same is true with us. Continue to become a person of the Word, a person of truth, and spotting the counterfeit lies of the devil becomes much, much easier. Staying faithful in our time with God each day allows you to "spot the not"–to discern the lies of the enemy.

Summary: Playground #2 of the enemy is deception. Our weapon is the Word of God. Overcome the devil's lies with the truth of God's Word!

3. Get your weaknesses under the covering of God.

We've looked at two weapons, or two playgrounds, of the devil so far. The first is doubt. The second is deception. And now the third is spiritual dullness. Dullness may not sound like a deeply spiritual word but look at 1 Peter 5:8 and pay careful attention to the first sentence.

> 1 Peter 5:8 *"Be alert and of sober mind*. Your enemy
> the devil prowls around like a roaring lion looking
> for someone to devour (italics added).

It's easy to jump ahead to the part about the devil being like a prowling lion ready to devour someone. But we must look at what comes before this powerful description of the devil. Peter tells us to be alert, sober minded, on guard, and on careful watch over our life. In other words, he is telling us to remain spiritually sharp. The truth is, God has called us to be the tip of the spear in His kingdom, not a dull butter knife with no spiritual effectiveness!

One way we become dull in our faith is by not surrendering certain areas of weakness to the Lord. God is masterful at transforming areas of weaknesses in our lives into strengths. The Holy Spirit is at work within us looking to strengthen the weaknesses in our lives that make us vulnerable to enemy attack. But when we refuse to surrender to this work, we become spiritually weak, dull, and ineffective. And this is where the rest of 1 Peter 5:8 comes into play. The devil is described as a lion looking for someone to devour. When we study the characteristics of a lion's attack, we come to realize that the primary way in which they attack a herd is by picking off the weakest member that has fallen behind from the rest of the pack. (Remember the chapter on church attendance? There is safety in numbers within the body of Christ!) Once separated and isolated, the lion strikes and sinks its teeth into the weak and defenseless animal.

Our areas of weaknesses will become the enemy's first point of attack against us. This is why we must allow God to do what He did for the great men and women of faith found in Hebrews 11:34,

> *"whose weakness was turned to strength*; and who became powerful in battle and routed foreign armies" (Italics added).

This is one of my life verses. It tells us that our weaknesses, frailties, and insecurities can be turned into strengths when we fully surrender them to the Lord. Through our own victory, we will teach and therefore release others to walk in their own freedom!

Summary: Playground #3 of the devil is dullness. We overcome this by remaining spiritually sharp by remaining surrendered before the Lord.

4. Set your heart on obedience.
Doubt. Deception. Dullness. We conclude with disobedience. This is the fourth playground where the devil loves to play. The Bible tells us that when we dwell in the land of disobedience, we give ground to the enemy to wreak havoc in our lives. Look at Ephesians 4:27,

> "and do not give the devil a foothold."

Footholds can quickly become strongholds of the enemy. Here is the progression. We first allow sin to have a toehold. We flirt with sin, thinking that just a little is ok. We ignore the warning of verses such as 1 Corinthians 5:6,

"A little yeast ruins the whole batch of dough"

The illustration is clear. Just a little bit of compromise can lead us into a whole lot of trouble. A little toehold can lead to a foothold and a foothold can then lead to a stronghold. A stronghold is just what it sounds like. It is something that has a strong hold over us. If you are struggling with sin, I would encourage you to re-read chapter 8 as a starting point toward freedom. But let me share one more verse with you that helps to guard our hearts from disobedience that can turn into a need for deliverance. 2 Timothy 2:22 says,

"Flee the evil desires of youth and pursue righteousness, faith, love and peace, along with those who call on the Lord out of a pure heart."

The answer to avoiding the extreme dangers of flirting with disobedience is to flee even the very desire for sin in the first place. The easiest way to do that is by taking our thoughts captive and engaging in an intentional pursuit of everything God calls good and Holy. When we do these things, we refuse to give the devil a foothold.

Summary: Disobedience is the fourth and final playground of the enemy. If he can get us to flirt with sin, he can establish a foothold in our life that could very well lead to a stronghold. The answer is to flee from evil desires by intentionally pursuing what God calls good and Holy.

Conclusion

Doubt. Deception. Dullness. Disobedience. These are four of the playgrounds of the enemy. I don't know about you, but I do not want to play on those playgrounds! They restrain us, quench what God has for us, and confine us to what I simply refer to as lower level living.

Jesus came to destroy the works of the devil and to set us free from the power and influence of the enemy. He has given us weapons of our warfare, four of which I've outlined for you in this chapter, to make sure that the release of God prevails over the restraint of the enemy. Let's yield to the One who lives in us and let us resist the enemy of our soul. For when we resist him, we are then able to release the life of God within us to others through our gifts, talents, and abilities.

Week 12 Spiritual Workout

- I am a big believer in journaling. When we write out what we are discovering about God, ourselves, and our life, dots are connected in powerful ways. Spend a little time reflecting on and journaling about the following:

One area of my life in which I doubt God is:

_____

_____

_____

_____

One lie the devil always seems to whisper in my ear is:

_____

_____

_____

_____

One sin I struggle with is: (And how would you categorize the struggle? Toehold, foothold, or stronghold?)

_____

_____

_____

_____

Which of the four weapons from this chapter do you need to apply a little more to your life?

_____

_____

_____

_____

- Secondly, for your Bible reading this week, we are going to start reading the book of Romans. Read Romans 1-3 and do one IRA. Practice praying using the PRAY acronym.

- Read the next chapter in this book.

Reflection Questions For Individual Or Small Group Use

1. What is one "DGRS" of the devil he tends to use against you the most? Is there anything from the journal exercise above that you need to share with another person or your small group as a point of insight and accountability?

2. Doubt. Deception. Dullness. Disobedience. Which of these four playgrounds do you tend to struggle with the most?

3. What spiritual weapon have you successfully used when over-coming the schemes of the enemy? Is there a spiritual weapon you need to sharpen that is kind of dull right now in this season of your life?

SECTION 5

Welcome to section 5 of Inside Out! I applaud you for making it this far!

So far, we have explored:

- **C**onnecting with God

- **O**ffering God everything

- **R**eleasing our ministry

Now we turn our hearts to look at:

- **E**ngaging in personal outreach and missions.

Remember, we have been engaging in a spiritual workout from the inside out. This last section is about as "out" as we can get because we are talking about reaching those who do not know Jesus and how to disciple them.

Chapter 13—Inside-Out Evangelism (The simple gospel: He came. He died. He rose again)

Chapter 14—Inside-Out Searching (Conversational evangelism)

Chapter 15—Inside-Out Missions (God's Call to Win the World)

Everything we have studied so far points us to this final CORE commitment of the Christian faith. We should connect with God, offer Him our everything, and learn to release our ministry so that we can give Jesus away to a lost and dying world.

Engaging in outreach personally and participating in world missions on some level is one of the most fulfilling, thrilling, and challenging disciplines of the Christian faith. Together, the body of Christ can fulfill the Great Commission Jesus spoke about in Mark 16:15 and Matthew 28:18-20. Let's look at these two passages:

> Mark 16:15 He said to them, "Go into all the world
> and preach the gospel to all creation.

> Matthew 28:18-20 18 Then Jesus came to them and said, "All
> authority in heaven and on earth has been given to me. 19

Therefore go and make disciples of all nations, baptizing them in
the name of the Father and of the Son and of the Holy Spirit, 20
and teaching them to obey everything I have commanded you.
And surely I am with you always, to the very end of the age."

You and I can present the message of the gospel to others, lead them to the Lord, and disciple them into spiritually mature Christ followers. This is the ultimate goal of the Christian faith and the greatest life mission we will ever fulfill while on this earth. And it is the reason the church exists in the first place!

I happen to believe that the gospel, which means good news, is still good and the Great Commission is still great. What God has done in our lives is still the greatest story we will ever tell someone else; therefore, we need to learn to do it clearly, compassionately, and convincingly. So, let's jump into this section and discover how to put a voice to the faith we so deeply cherish.

CHAPTER 13

Inside-Out Evangelism

Let me ask you a series of questions and see if you can you relate on any level:

Have you ever tried to invite someone to church and completely wimped out?

Have you ever tried to share your faith with someone, and a wall of fear crept up and sabotaged your efforts?

Have you ever tried to share something God has done in your life with someone who isn't saved and afterward felt like a complete idiot?

If you answered yes to any of the above questions, I assure you, you are not alone! I've experienced all three of the above scenarios myself. However, personal outreach and evangelism is a skill you can learn and is one of the most exciting things you can do as a believer. I have also discovered that nothing will light your faith on fire more than reaching others. In this chapter we are going to look at some simple principles for sharing our faith. They boil down to prayer and learning to present the gospel clearly.

Prayer

First, we need to understand that reaching others is a spiritual exercise. Paul said in 2 Corinthians 4:4,

> "The god of this age has blinded the minds of unbelievers,
> so that they cannot see the light of the gospel that displays
> the glory of Christ, who is the image of God."

The god of this age referred to in this passage is the devil and he has blinded the spiritual eyes of our unchurched friends from understanding clearly the saving grace of Jesus Christ. Furthermore, the Bible teaches us that the lost are the property of the devil, belonging to the kingdom of darkness, and are spiritually dead. Now let me ask you, does it sound like we need God to break through and do something in the midst of our efforts to reach a spiritually lost person? You bet. And that begins with prayer.

Let me revisit the story of my efforts to reach my parents and sister when I first got saved. I did everything I could, in my own power, to lead them to Jesus. I remember one time locking my parents in their bedroom and telling them they couldn't leave until they said the sinner's prayer. That didn't go over very well! On the heels of all my efforts, I distinctly remember the day I felt the Holy Spirit impress the thought upon my heart, "Why don't you just pray for your mom for a season before saying anything to her again?"

God spoke this to me as I was preparing to go on my first missions trip to Columbia. I was brand new to my youth group, but somehow got elected to play the role of Jesus in the human videos we would present to the children overseas. We practiced and practiced and practiced sharing the gospel overseas in public through drama, but privately I was praying and praying and praying for my mom during that window of time.

About 30 days prior to leaving for Columbia the Holy Spirit spoke to me that my mom needed a breakthrough when it came to understanding God's love for her. The only way I could verbalize the prayer was, "God, open up my mom's eyes to how much you love her." I prayed this simple prayer time and time again and said nothing to her about

Jesus. The only thing I did do was to invite her to come and watch us perform our dramas on the Sunday night service upon our return from Columbia. In fact, we were scheduled to fly in on Sunday afternoon and go straight to the church to perform our dramas and share about the trip during our evening service. And so here I am on the middle of the stage, having done this same drama a gazillion times in Columbia over the past week, and hoping that my mom would come watch this final presentation. In fact, to be honest, I remember "peeking" while being crucified in the middle of our church's stage to see if my mom was in the audience. Sure enough, she slipped into the church and sat down on the back row. I now did those dramas like it was the very first time!

After the dramas were over, I looked into the crowd and didn't see my mom. I believe she slipped out right as I was done, but at least she came. I went home exhausted yet fulfilled and collapsed on my bed. I was about to hit deep sleep mode when my dad knocked on my door and said, "You need to go outside to the carport. Your mother is crying and wants you." I can't tell you what all went through my head during the 45 seconds it took me to get outside. Was she suicidal again? Had she relapsed back into alcohol? I came out of the door and sure enough, she was weeping, but I could quickly discern they were tears of a different kind. She looked at me and said, "Tonight, the most amazing thing happened. I came to your church to see you do your dramas but something else happened as well." And then she said the exact same thing I had been praying over her for the previous 30 days. She said, "Mike, tonight it was as though Jesus himself came to me and opened my eyes to how much he loves me!" I couldn't believe it. My prayer had been answered! She went on to tell me that she had given her life to Christ before leaving the church. Glory! Several months later, my dad walked the aisle in that same church with tears rolling down his cheeks and surrendered his life to Jesus as well. I'm still to this day praying for my sister to come to know Jesus, but I know that at some point God will break through to her as well.

What is my point in sharing this long story? Evangelism begins with prayer. Are you praying for the unchurched people you are trying to reach? Right now, let me ask you to stop and think about one person in your life that does not know Christ and challenge you to pray for them.

Be sure to start off by asking the Holy Spirit to lead you in how to pray for them specifically. Write their name in the blank below and then the specific prayer you will pray over them for the next 30 days:

Person's name I am praying for: _____

Key prayer I am praying: _____

Present the gospel clearly

The time will come when you must not only pray for your unchurched friends but open your mouth and share the gospel with them. Romans 10:14-15 says, "How, then, can they call on the one they have not believed in? And how can they believe in the one of whom they have not heard? And how can they hear without someone preaching to them?" Read that last sentence again.

Our unchurched friends will never hear about Jesus unless some-one preaches to them. To preach does not mean you stand on the lunch table in the break room at work with slicked back hair, thump your friends over the head with a Bible, and preach fire and brimstone. Please don't do that. (Or wear your hair like that.)

To preach to your friends simply means to present Jesus to them in a way they can understand Him. I love what Paul said in Colossians 4:3-4,

"And pray for us, too, that God may open a door for our message, so that we may proclaim the mystery of Christ, for which I am in chains. *Pray that I may proclaim it clearly*, as I should" (Italics added).

This is a prayer we can all echo when trying to reach our friends for Christ. In fact, when you are praying for them like I mentioned above, pray these two things for yourself as well. First, pray that God would open a door for you to share with them. Secondly, pray that when He opens the door you will have the courage to share the gospel clearly with them.

One of my passions is communication and I am trying more and more to keep it simple when teaching others to communicate, espe-cially when it comes to sharing their faith. The simplest and clearest way

I can encourage you to share the story of Jesus is to remember three key phrases:

- He came

- He died

- He rose again.

If you can say, "He came," "He died," and He rose again," you can share the gospel with anyone!

He came– "Searching"
First "He came." Why? Because the Bible is clear that Jesus was on a search and rescue mission for you and me. Luke 19:10 says, "For the Son of Man came to seek and save the lost." That is the very reason Jesus came. He came seeking those who were lost (estranged from God) and spiritually dead because of their sin. Romans 6:23 says, "For the wages of sin is death, but the gift of God is eternal life in Christ Jesus our Lord." What you and I deserve because of our sin is spiritual death and that is exactly the starting point for every person on the planet. Jesus came to rescue us from this spiritual death. That is why He came. The key word you need to remember when you tell your friends "He came" is "searching." Because of His own love God came searching for you and me.

He died– "Sin"
Secondly, he died. Why did he die? Because as we just mentioned, the wages we deserve for our sin is spiritual death. Jesus came to take this death upon himself by dying an excruciating death on a Roman torture device known as a cross. By doing so, he paid the debt that you and I deserve to pay, and He paid this spiritual debt in full! His dying on the cross was the ultimate expression of His love for us. John 3:16 says "For God so loved the world (insert your name here) that He gave His one and only Son that whosoever believes in Him shall not perish but have everlasting life" (parenthesis added). Make no mistake about it. God loves you and He proved it by loving you to the point of death. The key word to remember when you tell someone He died is "sin." Jesus had

to die in order to pay the debt caused by our sin. So, let's review.... He came searching for the lost. He died to pay the price for our sin.

He rose again

But that's not all. He rose again. Three days after his crucifixion, Jesus experienced a glorious resurrection. The Bible says that God exerted His power in Christ and raised Him back to the life. This is crucial to the Christian faith. In fact, there is no Christianity without an empty tomb. Why? First, Jesus promised that He would be raised to life. His resurrection is a matter of His credibility. But secondly, his resurrection is a matter of him defeating death, both physical and spiritual, once and for all. Through His resurrection He provided a way for us to come back alive spiritually. Whereas the cross is about forgiveness of our sins, the resurrection is about our new life. The Bible says that when we accept Christ as our Lord and Savior, the same Spirit that raised Christ from the dead, the Holy Spirit we have talked about all through the pages of this book, comes inside of us and brings us back to life spiritually. This is why Jesus said in John 3:3, "No one comes to the Father unless He is born again." When we surrender our lives to Christ, the Spirit of God comes inside of us and brings spiritual life to us as a brand-new child of God. Therefore, the key word when communicating He rose again is "surrender."

So, let's review

- He came – The key word is "searching."

- He died – The key word is "sin."

- He rose again – The key word is "surrender."

Conclusion

That's it. That's the gospel. He came seeking the spiritually dead. That's every person on the planet when they are born due to the original sin of Adam and Eve in the garden. He died to pay the penalty for our sin. And He rose again so that we can be spiritually alive and become a child of God. Can you communicate that? Absolutely. Can you memorize a few verses to help you along the way? Sure you can. Can you put it in your own words and communicate Jesus clearly to others? I have no doubt that you can. For now, pray in the same manner Paul prayed in

Colossians 4, "God help me to communicate the gospel clearly. You came, you died, and you rose again for me and for the person I am trying to reach!"

Week 13 Spiritual Workout

- From this point forward, continue to pray for the unreached person in your life that you listed above. In fact, you may want to rework your daily prayer plan that you developed in chapter five to include praying for the lost people in your life. This can include your lost friend, your community, your nation, and unreached people groups around the world.

- Read Romans 4-6 and do one IRA. Practice praying using the PRAY acronym.

- Read the next chapter in this book.

Reflection Questions For Individual Or Small Group Use

1. Why are Christians scared to share their faith? Share about a time when you gave into fear and didn't follow through on your attempt to reach someone. Share about a time when you pressed beyond that wall of fear in order to share the gospel.

2. Which of the three aspects of the gospel (He came, He died, He rose again) may be more of a struggle for you to communicate to others? Do you have any questions about any of these three concepts?

3. How do you feel about the role of the Holy Spirit in sharing our faith? Do you believe God will speak to you about how to pray and what to say to the lost people in your life?

CHAPTER 14

Inside Out Searching (Reaching One Person At A Time)

Luke 19:10 says, "Jesus came to seek and to save the lost." He came to this earth on a search and rescue mission for humanity. And in the early stages of his ministry, the result of his mission caused many to search for Him.

John 6:24 gives us a fascinating glimpse into the impact that Jesus was having on the crowds through his ministry on earth.

"Once the crowd realized that neither Jesus nor his disciples were there, they got into the boats and went to Capernaum *in search of Jesus*" (italics added).

I love the last part of that verse, "in search of Jesus." The truth is, I believe there are lost people in our lives who, deep down, are searching for something deeper to fulfill them. Some are attempting to find this fulfillment through sin and the world in which we live. Others are at the point where they realize there must be something better than what this world has to offer but have no idea where to find it. That's where we come in to present the three points of the gospel we explored in the last chapter (He came, He died, He rose again).

In this chapter, I want to offer you some further help with practical and conversational evangelism. In John chapter 4, Jesus presents Himself to someone who is known as the woman at the well. If we are going to learn how to present Jesus, we might as well learn from an example where Jesus presented Himself! Let's break down this story verse by verse and glean some great insight into the nature of sharing Christ with others.

Note: I realize that conversations rarely flow as simply as the one we are about to read. Conversations ebb and flow, but the principles and strategies within this chapter will give us some practical reference points we can use as we endeavor to share our faith.

So pause for a second, take your Bible out, and read John 4:1-42. Following are some insights we can glean from this story.

We must make a conscience decision to move beyond our inconvenience.

Verse 4 says, "Now He had to go through Samaria." I believe this verse reveals more than just a geographical issue. Perhaps Jesus had to go through Samaria in order to reach his final destination. However, there is something deeper here that is supported by 2 Peter 3:9 which says that God is not willing that any should perish but that all come to repentance. Therefore, He is willing to do anything to reach people with His grace and truth. In this passage, it meant Jesus going through Samaria.

In Biblical days, Jews and Samaritans didn't speak. Cultural norms would require Jews to travel around Samaria to avoid going through it. Men were also never to initiate conversation with women as Jesus did in this passage. Yet Jesus "had to go through Samaria." Why? Because he isn't willing that anyone should perish.

We must also be willing to overcome our own inconveniences and hindrances when it comes to reaching people. We must be willing to move through our fear, pride, insecurity, and even our lack of knowledge when it comes to sharing Jesus with others. 2 Corinthians 5:14 says, "For Christ's love compels us, for we are convinced that one died for all." We need to become compelled by the love of Christ to the point that we too go through our own Samaria.

We must establish common ground.

Verse 6 says, "He sat down." Sure, Jesus was tired from the journey, but him sitting down to speak with this woman communicates another pivotal concept about reaching people. Jesus sat down in order to get on her level, and we must do the same. We sit down, or get on the same level with the people we are trying to reach, by establishing common ground with them. This is where the relational aspect of outreach comes into play. It is spending time with people on common turf—eating lunch together, playing ball together, going to the gym together, having coffee together, and the list goes on and on. Build a relationship with the people you are trying to reach through the common ground you share. And allow this friendship to naturally become a platform to share your faith.

We must ask good questions.

Verse 7 says, "Will you give me a drink?" Jesus asked a question when trying to reach the woman at the well. That very question would become the basis of him sharing eternal truth with her, but at first it was just a simple question.

I promise you, if we would learn to ask good questions and become good listeners, we will greatly influence people with the gospel. For starters, when we ask questions, we place ourselves in the position of genuinely taking interest in others. Our care for others becomes the basis of our credibility when sharing spiritual truths. As it has been said, "people don't care how much you know until they know how much you care." This concept is Biblical and believe it or not starts by asking genuine questions.

We must realize, however, that the kinds of questions we ask can determine the level of influence we gain with a person. For example, there is a difference between a "what" question and a "how" question. "What" questions could include:

- What are you doing this weekend?

- What project are you currently working on at work?

- What sports do your kids play?

- What are your hobbies?

"What" questions are great to ask when you are getting to know someone. But the next level are "how" questions. They lend themselves to deeper levels of conversation and expand the platform to share your faith. Questions like:

- How are your kids doing?

- How are you doing with all the stress at work?

- How's the marriage going?

- How can I be praying for you?

When first trying to reach someone, start with the "what" questions. But as you build a friendship, move into the "how" questions. When you do, you will begin to see one opportunity after another open up for you to insert your faith in the conversation.

We must turn the natural into the spiritual.
Verse 10 says, "Jesus answered her, 'If you knew the gift of God and who it is that asks you for a drink, you would have asked him, and he would have given you living water.' Jesus took something in the natural, water, and turned it into a spiritual conversation by calling himself "living water." When we start moving beyond our internal fear and start asking "how" questions that express genuine interest in a person, we will have ample opportunity to pivot the conversation from the natural to the spiritual in a seamless way. Take for example, one of the above how questions from our list and see how it could play out:

- You: "How are your kids doing?"

- Your friend, in frustration says: "Man, they are acting like little hellions lately. I don't know what I'm going to do with these kids!"

At this point, you can turn this conversation to the spiritual:

- You: "That's tough. Let me ask you, do you have your kids in some kind of church youth group or kids' program? I sure have found that this helps with my kids." This is called a bridge statement or question. It serves to build a bridge between the natural and the spiritual.

- Your friend: "No, we aren't really church goers."

This is a scenario that could easily play out with one of your friends. And all you have to do is build a bridge by connecting something they say with something that could open up a doorway for spiritual conversation. Bridge statements are also useful when your friend expresses pain of some kind. For example, if a co-worker is majorly stressed and either blows up in anger or breaks down in tears, you can easily come to them after they calm down and say something like, "You are obviously stressed. You ok? I'm available if you need to talk. I'll also keep you in prayer if you are ok with that." Just say it and see what happens. The cracked door could turn into a wide-open opportunity. You could even find yourself praying with them right there on the spot!

We must present Jesus.
John 4:13-14 says, "Jesus answered, 'Everyone who drinks this water will be thirsty again, but whoever drinks the water I give them will never thirst. Indeed, the water I give them will become in them a spring of water welling up to eternal life.' This is Jesus' gospel presentation unfolding before us. In order for the gospel presentation to unfold between us and our friends, I suggest asking a question of permission. Let me insert this question of permission into the conversation with our imaginary friend that we started from above. It will be in bold:

- You: "How are your kids doing?"

- Your friend, in frustration says: "Man, they are acting like little hellions lately. I don't know what I'm going to do with these kids!"

- You: "Man, that's tough. Let me ask you, do you have your kids in some kind of church youth group or kids' program? I sure have found that this helps with my kids."

- Your friend: "No, we aren't really church goers."

- You: "That's cool. At one point I wasn't a church goer either. **Do you mind if I share with you three quick reasons why I go to church in the first place?"**

Hopefully your friend will say....

- Your friend: "Sure, I guess."

- You: "Cool, I'll be brief. When I was 24 years old, I came to understand three things about Jesus Christ. First, he came to this earth searching for me in order to bring me back into relationship with the Father. Second, the reason I was lost in the first place was because of my sin. The Bible says, "the wages of sin is death," which is eternal separation from God. But Jesus died on the cross to take my place and pay the penalty I deserve. And thirdly, He rose again after His crucifixion. The God of the Bible is alive and desires to have a relationship with me. I started this relationship when I surrendered my life to Him in college."

And then ask another pivotal question: "Have you ever considering starting a relationship with God because of what Christ did for you?"

Boom! You just presented the gospel simply and clearly! And you've placed the ball in their court. You've left them with some decisions to make about the gospel. But don't stop there!

We must not back down.
In the course of Jesus' conversation with this lady at the well, something profound occurs. Let's keep breaking down our story and look at verses 15-17. The woman said to him, "Sir, give me this water so that I won't get thirsty and have to keep coming here to draw water." He told her, "Go, call your husband and come back." "I have no husband," she replied. Jesus said to her, "You are right when you say you have no husband. The fact is, you have had five husbands, and the man you now have is not your husband. What you have just said is quite true."

Two profound things happened here:

- **Jesus relied on the Holy Spirit**—this woman did not outright tell Jesus that she was living in adultery. The Spirit of God revealed this to Jesus. Ok, connect the dots with me here from our last section. Remember the spiritual gifts we talked about? They can also be exercised to reach lost people. The truth is, the Spirit of God within us knows how to reach a person better than we do. The Spirit knew the prayer I should pray for my mother. And the Holy Spirit knows what is really taking place in the life of every non-believer that He is trying to draw to the Father. There are many great gospel presentation techniques out there you can learn, but don't forget about the Holy Spirit as you are engaging in conversation. He will help direct your thoughts, your words, and the angle you take to share the gospel. And yes, the Spirit of God can also reveal something to you about the person in order to reveal just how real He is—so stay dependent upon the Spirit when you share your faith!

- **Jesus wasn't afraid to address the sin issue**—and neither should we be afraid to do the same. The truth is, this woman's adultery would be a stumbling block to her turning the reigns of her life fully over to Jesus. And unless our friends are willing to repent of sin, they simply cannot be saved. It's not that they sign up to be perfect overnight, but there has to be an awareness within them that sin is the root issue as to why we are separated from God in the first place and that, in order to be saved, we must turn from sin and allow Jesus to be Lord of our life. So don't back down. Jesus didn't and neither should we. Speak the truth in love, but by all means, speak the truth about the very reason we are lost in the first place which is sin.

We must lead them in a prayer of faith.

The woman acknowledged that there was something special about Jesus. v. 19 "Sir," the woman said, "I can see that you are a prophet." Jesus went on to share with her that He was more than a prophet. He was indeed the Messiah who came into the world to save people. Sometimes all we do is move the needle spiritually for people as we present the gospel. They may come to say, "I can see Jesus is a good teacher" but aren't quite ready yet to say, "Jesus is Lord of my life." And if that's the case, no problem. They've moved forward. But there will be times when we present the gospel, that someone is ready to receive Jesus as He is— Lord. When that is the case, it will be obvious. The next step at that point is simply leading them in a short prayer that goes something like this:

"Dear Jesus, thank you for coming to this earth searching for me and thank you for dying on the cross for my sins. Forgive me of my sins and come into my life as my Savior and my Lord. By faith I receive heaven as a gift you paid for and I surrender my life to you. Help me to live for you all the days of my life. In Jesus' name, amen!"

Conclusion

One last time let me remind you that real life conversations, and real time situations with people ebb and flow and jump all over the place. It would be easy to read a chapter like this and expect conversations to flow in a linear fashion with no rabbit trails, no interruptions, and no questions asked. But we all know it doesn't always happen that way. However, keep this story of Jesus and the woman at the well in mind as you share your faith with other people.

- Build a relationship with the unchurched through common ground.

- Learn to ask "what" and "how" questions. Determine to become a good listener and express genuine care and concern.

- Take a bold step and make a bridge statement and see if the conversation turns into a spiritual one.

- Courageously ask a pivoting question.

- Present the gospel using the three statements we have been discussing—he came searching, he died for our sin, he rose again, and we must surrender to Him as Lord in order to be saved.

- Learn a simple sinner's prayer that you can pray with people who are ready to receive Christ.

But above all, remain dependent upon the Holy Spirit. Again, He will lead you as you attempt to reach your unsaved friends and even speak to you on their behalf. And lastly, take a deep breath, relax, and just do it. Sharing our faith is a spiritual muscle we must work out. But as we do, we will see God honoring the steps we take to reach someone, and we will become a stronger witness to others. Remember, the good news is still good, and the Great Commission is still great!

Week 14 Spiritual Workout

- Continue to pray for the unchurched person you listed above. This week, however, go to the next level and make every effort to share more of your faith with them. Commit to put the evangelism skills we covered in this chapter into practice with one of your unchurched friends and be ready to share this experience with your small group or another believer.

- Read Romans 7-9 and do one IRA. Practice praying using the PRAY acronym.

- Read the next chapter in this book.

Reflection Questions For Individual Or Small Group Use

1. What is the common ground that you share with at least one lost person in your life?

2. What are some other "what" questions and "how questions" you can ask the lost people in your life?

3. What are some other examples of bridge statements you can make to turn a natural conversation into a spiritual one?

CHAPTER 15

Inside-Out Missions

Let's read two Bible verses and you tell me the one word that is in both verses:

> John 3:16 "For God so loved the world that he gave
> His one and only Son that whosoever believes in Him
> shall not perish but have everlasting life."

Mark 16:15 "Go into all the world and preach the good news."

Did you catch the common word in both of these famous passages of Scripture? That's right—world. The bottom line is that Jesus came into the world in order to reach the world.

For God so loved the world that He gave his one and only Son—yet half of the world has yet to hear a clear presentation of the gospel of Jesus Christ. Think about that for just a minute. There are 6 billion people on the planet and 3 billion of them have yet to hear about the eternal hope that Jesus offers through His death and resurrection. We must continue to do our part in fulfilling the Great Commission. We must continue to do our part in reaching the world. And by world, I mean here, there, and everywhere.

Here, there, everywhere

Let's look one more time at Acts 1:8:

> "But you will receive power when the Holy Spirit comes on you; and you will be my witnesses in Jerusalem, and in all Judea and Samaria, and to the ends of the earth."

This verse says that the same Spirit who works within us from the inside out will also help us reach all people—from the ones we work with every day to the people who live on the other side of the planet that we will never see in our lifetime. Evangelism is truly here, there, and everywhere. Jesus described this truth by telling us we would be witnesses in three spheres of influence:

- In Jerusalem—For those hearing this passage when it was originally spoken, Jerusalem was the most immediate area where they were gathered. For us, our Jerusalem consists of those people we see every day who do not know Jesus—our friends, family, co-workers, classmates, and neighbors. This is our *here*.

- In Samaria—This was the geographical region surrounding Jerusalem. For us, our Samaria represents our community, our city, and the region our local church is called to reach. This is our *there*.

- The ends of the earth—This is the same for us as it was those who originally heard Acts 1:8. We are called to reach the ends of the earth through the gospel of Jesus Christ. God desires that our church and even our individual lives impacts the world—this is our *everywhere*. But how?

The last two chapters were essentially a means to reach our "here"—the people closest to us each day who do not know Christ. But how are we to reach the ends of the earth? There are two simple ways—through our going and our giving.

Note: Although I'm not addressing how to reach our cities in this section, I have developed a campaign with our communities in mind called Reach the City. You can check it out at www.reachthecity.com

Our going—We can reach the ends of the earth by going on a short-term missions trip

Stay with me for a moment and allow me to share something humorous that happened to me on another missions trip to South America. It wasn't humorous at the time, but it sure is now.

I was so excited I couldn't sleep. It was the night before we left for the trip and I couldn't wait to fly again to tell people about Jesus in another country. Our missions team had practiced our human videos a million times.

I literally pulled an all-nighter in my excitement but reasoned that I would be able to sleep during the 12-hour bus ride to Miami, Florida before flying out. But nope, I didn't sleep at all. Surely, I would sleep during the overnight plane trip but guess what, I couldn't sleep on the plane either. I was literally awake for 72 hours before getting one minute of sleep in a third world hotel we called home for the week. But the hotel itself became an adventure when the alarms started to sound. Panic struck the hallways, and Latin American people started screaming in Spanish. None of us white American kids could understand until a translator was able to make out one word, "EARTHQUAKE!" Everybody started to run to the doorways of the hotel because supposedly that is the safest place in such an emergency. Items fell off the wall and the 10-story hotel began to sway back and forth under the magnitude of the earthquake. (I love roller coasters but to this day no ride has ever been able to top this experience!)

The next day the city was placed under martial law and we couldn't leave the hotel for 36 hours. We looked out of the hotel and saw police and militia with machine guns on the street. We did our entire ministry program over and over again for the hotel guests and staff as we were all locked in the hotel and were prohibited to leave. This all happened on one of my first missions trips and nothing like it has happened on one since. But I am here to tell you, I would not trade that experience for anything in the world because there is simply nothing like going overseas and telling others about Christ.

As a pastor, I have cast a vision for my people to go on an overseas mission trip once every four years. As a church, we provide one trip a year and we rotate between a stateside trip and an overseas trip. That means we provide an overseas opportunity every two years. One of our goals is for every young person in our church to go on an overseas trip before they graduate from high school and we are becoming increasingly more intentional in our endeavor to reach this goal. I am not sure what your church does to foster mission opportunities, but there are plenty of reputable organizations out there eager for partners to join with them. Here are four quick reasons why experiencing missions overseas is so important:

- **Our worldview is challenged.** Experiencing and witnessing first-hand the poverty and darkness that people in other countries are living in highlights how blessed we are to live in America. Staying close to the Holy Spirit while on a mission trip increases compassion for the lost in deeper and more profound, and often heartbreaking, ways. This, in and of itself, will change your life.

- **Our comfort zone is stretched, and that's always a good thing.** Leaving behind the familiar can be an uncomfortable experience as is being pushed to the edge of ourselves – physically, emotionally, and even spiritually. But this push, if we allow it, will push us and the team we are with to lean into God like never before. And when this happens, we see Him show up in miraculous ways. I've seen it time and time again.

- **Our gifts are used outside of our normal context.** Whether it is loving on poor children, teaching English as a second language, or building a church with bare hands, there is something special and unique about using our God given abilities overseas. For one thing, motives are purified, and our abilities and gifts are used for the people God cares about the most—those who do not know Him. For another, there is a clearer realization of just how much the Holy Spirit is needed to help fulfill the tasks at hand while serving on the trip. This dependency on the Holy Spirit will only further the development of the talents we have been given.

- **Our eyes witness salvation!** People are saved. Is there any greater benefit? Seeing someone come to Christ in an overseas context is so heart stirring and impactful, often in ways that it is not when we see someone walk to the altar in an American church. Maybe it shouldn't, but it often does strike a deeper chord within us as we realize the truth of John 3:16, "for God so loved the world "and see it revealed right before our eyes. There is a greater understanding of why Jesus came to this earth and why we should all go to the four corners of the world to reach people.

The bottom line is that Jesus came into the world to reach the entire world and He has chosen to do so through you and me. Imagine that! God has left the most important task on the planet, the evangelization of the world, in our hands to fulfill through the power of the Holy Spirit. How humbling, how exciting, and how awesome is such a task. I challenge you to go on an overseas mission trip. It will change your own world as you attempt to reach the world!

Giving—We can reach the ends of the earth through our sacrificial giving.

Even though we can't always go on a missions trip, we can always give financially in order to fund global outreach. In fact, one of the greatest investments we can ever make is into the missions program of our local church or denomination. In chapter 9 we looked at stewarding our finances well and the principle of tithing. However, not every believer who attends a local church tithes. In fact, in any given local church only 10-25% give a full 10% to the Lord as a true tithe. That means if you spread this 10-25% of faithful tithers across the entire body of Christ, the average Christian is only giving 2.5% of their income to the local church. That equates to a shortage of 7.5% out of 10% per person in every local church!

What would happen, however, if every person who attends church regularly would truly tithe? According to an article from Relevant Magazine*, the fruit would be astounding. If everyone who claimed to be a Christian would tithe there would be an additional $165 billion for churches to use and distribute. Just think what could be done to reach people with an additional $165 billion dollars. This same article tells us what could be accomplished with this extra money:

- $25 billion could relieve global hunger, starvation and deaths from preventable diseases in five years.

- $12 billion could eliminate illiteracy in five years.

- $15 billion could solve the world's water and sanitation issues, specifically at places in the world where 1 billion people live on less than $1 per day.

- $1 billion could fully fund all overseas mission work.

- $100 – $110 billion would still be left over for additional ministry expansion.

Wow. Staggering, isn't it? And this does not even include any additional offerings that many believers give above and beyond their tithe for the sake of missions. In my local context, we challenge our church to give monthly above their tithe in an offering to missions. And it has been amazing to see people give above and beyond their tithe to missions in a sacrificial yet joyful way.

This is not an attempt to twist your arm into giving. I just want to illustrate what could take place if everyone did their part financially in the body of Christ. How much more quickly could the church of Jesus Christ reach the world? How much more relevant could we become in our own communities as we meet the needs of people in our own backyard? How many impoverished lives, both physically and spiritually, could be impacted if we had the funding and resources necessary to bring hope to the hopeless? And finally, how much more quickly could we see the second return of Christ as a result of both our going and our giving to missions? It's time for us to go. It's time for us to give. It's time for us to do our part to reach our world—here, there, and everywhere.

Conclusion

This chapter concludes the primary content related to the four CORE disciplines of the Christian faith. But wait, there's more! I just posed a question above that I hope you noticed. I asked,

And finally, how much more quickly could we see the second return of Christ as a result of both our going and our giving to missions?

The return of Christ. No book on discipleship would be complete without talking about the second coming of Jesus and what will take place in the earth as that day approaches. Every believer must allow the hope of His return to shine brightly in their hearts and to know what will take place in the earth as we approach that glorious day. That's where we will begin our cool down section of this spiritual workout. And following that, we will discuss how you can disciple someone else into spiritual maturity. I hope you plan to hang with me through the end of the book. Trust me, you don't want to miss the content of the next chapter!

Week 15 Spiritual Workout

- This may seem like a strange exercise, but I want you to find a world map, lay your hands on it, and begin to pray. You could even print one off of the internet, but I want you to have a physical hard copy of a map that you can touch and feel. Each day for seven days, lay your hands on it during your quiet time and pray for the world. As you do so, ask God to give you a burden for certain regions of the world.

- Read Romans 10-12 and do an IRA.

- Read the next chapter in this book.

Reflection Questions For Individual Or Small Group Use

1. Where is one place in the world you would like to travel for an overseas mission trip?

2. If you have been on a mission trip before, reflect on this trip and write out some things you learned about God, yourself, and the world as a result of you going. Share these insights with a fellow believer or small group.

3. How do you as an individual (and how does your church) share the gospel here, there, and everywhere? What can you do to strengthen these efforts?

*https://relevantmagazine.com/love-and-money/
what-would-happen-if-church-tithed/

SECTION 6

Welcome to the last and final section of our spiritual workout together! We just finished up what might have felt like a marathon of spiritual content. The fact that you have made it this far and are still engaged with the material proves that you have what this last section is all about—endurance. That's right...endurance!

I realize that in keeping with the nature of a workout you are supposed to have a cool down after hitting the gym. That would mean this final section of our book should be a wind down, and it is, but not quite like you think. In the natural, a cool down suggests the workout is over and it is time to chill. But in the spiritual, we must understand that the only thing winding down is heaven's spiritual clock as we draw closer and closer to the return of Christ. And whereas we certainly need to learn how to find our rest in Christ and be at peace in Him, we must also maintain our sense of responsibility to continue in Christ until the very end and help others do the same.

Therefore, this section will cover three things:

Chapter 16—Inside Out Perseverance (The call to continue in the midst of the last days)

Chapter 17—Inside Out Discipleship (It's your turn—How to disciple others)

Chapter 18—Inside Out Life (Six ways we are called to do life with others)

As you read through this final section, let me remind you to remain faithful in your time with God. Continue to do the spiritual workouts provided at the end of each chapter and answer the reflection questions provided. Share your answers with a fellow believer you trust or your small group.

Let's finish this book strong and again, thank you for your commitment to journey with me to greater spiritual growth!

CHAPTER 16

Inside Out Perseverance

We must, as we've done this entire book, re-emphasize our CORE verse one more time.

> Philippians 2:12-13 "Therefore, my dear friends, as you have always obeyed—not only in my presence, but now much more in my absence—continue to work out your salvation with fear and trembling. For it is God who works in you to will and to act according to His good purpose."

Think back to what we discussed in chapter seven. When you see a "therefore" written in the Bible, read the verses preceding it to see what it is there for. Just before this passage in Philippians, Paul wrote that one day, "at the name of Jesus every knee should bow, in heaven and on earth and under the earth, and every tongue confess that Jesus Christ is Lord, to the glory of God the Father" (verses 10-11.)

Paul is referring to what will ultimately take place at the conclusion of a time known as the last days. The last days began when Jesus Christ returned to heaven after He was resurrected from the dead. Since his ascension, the heavens and earth have been on God's timetable, anxiously awaiting what is called the Second Coming of Christ. He came once to redeem mankind from sin, but he will come again to fulfill His redemptive plan throughout the earth. And Paul says, one day, every knee will bow and every tongue confess that Jesus is Lord. This means that for those of us who have already received Him as Lord, we will willingly bow our knees with heartfelt awe and worship. But for those who have not, they will bow their knees with the fear of judgment in their hearts.

And in light of this sobering truth, Paul says we must do one thing— wrapped up in one word. That word is "Continue…"

The entire call to work out our salvation with fear and trembling is essentially a call to continue in our faith until the very end. Let's also look at Colossians 2:6-7,

"So then, just as you received Christ Jesus as Lord, *continue* to live your lives in him, rooted and built up in him, strengthened in the faith as you were taught, and overflowing with thankfulness" (italics added.)

We must set our hearts on holding fast to our faith and remain faithful to the very end. We must continue to abide in Him and allow the Holy Spirit to empower us to finish strong from the inside out. To do so will ignite the eternal hope we have that this world is not our final home. Let's remain close to Him and allow our connection with God to fuel our commitment to Him in these final days. Now, let's dive into a very basic understanding of the second return of Christ.

That Glorious Day
The landmark verse of the New Testament that speaks about the return of Christ is 1 Thessalonians 4:16-17:

"For the Lord himself will come down from heaven with a loud command, with the voice of the archangel and with the trumpet call of God, and the dead in Christ will rise first. After that we who are still alive and are left will be caught up together with them in the clouds to meet the Lord in the air. And so we will be with the Lord forever."

The phrase used in this passage, "caught up together," is what is commonly referred to as the rapture of the church. It is the moment in which those believers who have died prior to Christ's second coming, as well as those believers who are currently living, are instantly taken to heaven to be with the Lord forever. This is known as our blessed hope (see Titus 2:13).

New Testament Christians lived their lives with great anticipation as though the return of Christ was imminent and could happen at any moment. We, too, are to live our lives in such a way. We are to serve Jesus and share Him as though today could be the day of His return. To live life and to serve the Lord from this paradigm literally keeps our eyes looking forward to heaven, our hearts filled with hope, and our feet to the floor when it comes to fulfilling the Great Commission.

But If you are newer to the faith, or newer to exploring the topic of the return of Christ, you might ask the same question that many, including myself, have asked. "Ok so, WHEN will His second coming take place?" Good question! Jesus addressed this very thing as well as many other issues relating to His second coming in Matthew 24. Look at what He specifically said concerning the timing in which He would come back in Matthew 24:36,

> "No one knows about that day or hour, not even the angels in heaven, nor the Son, but only the Father."

Jesus is clear. Only His Father knows the exact time He will motion to Jesus and release Him to go and get His church. In the meantime, we are to "Keep watch, because you do not know on what day your Lord will come" (Matthew 24:42). Elsewhere Jesus describes his coming as a surprise, comparing it to a "thief in the night,"–telling us that many will be caught off guard and end up being left behind at His coming. He gives an example of this sobering reality in Matthew 24:40-41,

> "Two men will be in the field; one will be taken and the other left. Two women will be grinding with a hand mill; one will be taken and the other left."

In other words, people will be going through the routines of their lives and suddenly Christ will return. His faithful followers will disappear to be with him, and those who are unbelievers will be left behind. Those who are raptured will receive transformed bodies and the bodies of believers who died before this event will rise as well and be caught up with Christ. Wow, that should cause us all to pause for a moment, survey our hearts, and make sure we take as many people with us as possible when God sounds the trumpet signaling the return of Jesus!

Signs

Even though we do not know the exact hour the rapture will take place, we understand from Scripture that there will definitely be signs indicating that this glorious moment is drawing near. Consider just two examples from the book of 1 & 2 Timothy. They boil down to two things: an erosion of truth and terrible times.

- **An erosion of truth**—1 Timothy 4:1-2 says, "The Spirit clearly says that in later times some will abandon the faith and follow deceiving spirits and things taught by demons. Such teachings come through hypocritical liars, whose consciences have been seared as with a hot iron."

- **Terrible times**—2 Timothy 3:1-5 says, "But mark this: There will be terrible times in the last days. People will be lovers of themselves, lovers of money, boastful, proud, abusive, disobedient to their parents, ungrateful, unholy, without love, unforgiving, slanderous, without self-control, brutal, not lovers of the good, treacherous, rash, conceited, lovers of pleasure rather than lovers of God— having a form of godliness but denying its power. Have nothing to do with such people.".

We will know the return of Christ is drawing near as we continue to see the unfolding of deception and wickedness on the earth. We will also continue to see terrible times in the earth. Matthew 24:6-8 says, "You will hear of wars and rumors of wars, but see to it that you are not alarmed. Such things must happen, but the end is still to come. Nation will rise against nation, and kingdom against kingdom. There will be famines and earthquakes in various places. All these are the beginning of birth pains."

One last sobering verse is one that Jesus said Himself in Matthew 24:12-13,

> "Because of the increase of wickedness, the love of most will grow cold, but the one who stands firm to the end will be saved."

The culmination of the signs of the times is that peoples' hearts will grow colder and colder to the things of God. Clearly, we must intentionally keep our hearts growing warmer and warmer in our love for the Lord! We must stand firm for Christ. We must persevere as disciples. And we must continue in our faith. Look at Romans 13:11-12,

> "And do this, understanding the present time: The hour has already come for you to wake up from your slumber, because our salvation is nearer now than when we first believed. The night is nearly over; the day is almost here. So let us put aside the deeds of darkness and put on the armor of light."

Paul instructs us to understand the present time called the last days, and to make sure we do not fall into spiritual slumber. We must not become lazy in our faith or embrace a laissez faire attitude toward Christ and the things He cares about the most. I love what Paul says in Romans 12:11, "Never be lacking in zeal, but keep your spiritual fervor, serving the Lord." We are to keep our love for Christ blazing hot and earnestly desire to fulfill the Great Commandment which is to, "Love the Lord your God with all your heart and with all your soul and with all your mind." (Matthew 22:37)

Of course, there is more we could understand about the end times and I would encourage you to dive into more research regarding things you may have heard about like the final judgement, the Great Tribulation, Armageddon, and the Millennial Reign. I would encourage you to talk through these other aspects of the last days with your mentor or your pastor and consider purchasing one of the many great study Bibles available today. But the most important thing is to keep growing spiritually. Remain faithful to attending church. Stay consistent with your quiet times. Grow with other believers in a small group. Read books by reputable authors on your own as you are able. And you will see that over time you will grow in your understanding of not only topics like the end days but many of the other wonderful facets of our faith.

One Last Promise

I know that chapters like this one that contain unfamiliar content can leave us feeling like a deer caught in the headlights. So let me encourage you with one of my favorite verses in the Bible. It is the last verse in the book of Jude. The book of Jude is right before the book of Revelation, which is the last book in the Bible and is filled with more information concerning the end times. Jude says in the final verse before the book of Revelation begins:

> "To him who is able to keep you from stumbling and to
> present you before his glorious presence without fault
> and with great joy—to the only God our Savior be glory,
> majesty, power and authority, through Jesus Christ our Lord,
> before all ages, now and forevermore! Amen" (V.24).

What a great promise to hang our faith on even in the midst of the last days that are full of trials. Jude points us right back to the blood of Jesus and the power of God within us. God, who dwells in us by the Holy Spirit, is able to keep us strong to the end and present us before the glorious presence of Jesus without fault and with great joy—from the inside out. So don't fret, just stay faithful. Let's continue to work out what God is working in us and let's help others do the same on a practical level. That is what the next chapter is all about, learning to disciple others so they too will remain strong in the last days.

Week 16 Spiritual Workout

- Finish the book of Romans, chapters 13-16, and do one IRA

- Pray and think about what you would like to do for your Bible reading beyond this week.

- Read the next chapter in this book.

Reflection Questions

1. What questions do you have about the Second Coming of Christ?

2. What are some other examples of the "signs of the times" that are taking place right before our very eyes?

3. What would be just one question you have about the events and timeline of the end days?

CHAPTER 17

Inside-Out Discipleship
(It's your turn—How to disciple others)

In chapter 13 I made the statement: "The good news is still GOOD." And it is. The good news of the gospel is still good and absolutely worth sharing with others.

In this chapter, however, allow me to make another statement that is equally true: The Great Commission is still GREAT!

The Great Commission of Jesus is found in Matthew 28:18-20:

> Then Jesus came to them and said, "All authority in heaven and on earth has been given to me. Therefore, go and make disciples of all nations, baptizing them in the name of the Father and of the Son and of the Holy Spirit, and teaching them to obey everything I have commanded you. And surely I am with you always, to the very end of the age."

Jesus spoke these words right before what is known as His ascension—His return to heaven. Jesus had come to earth in human form, died on a cross, and rose from the dead and was now about to return to His Father in heaven. But before doing so He gave His disciples the greatest responsibility known to mankind—making more disciples, or close followers of Jesus, across all nations.

He gave this command to the disciples who had become His followers during His ministry on earth intending that this Great Commission be carried on by every future generation. Whether you realize it or not, your own faith is a result of this Great Commission. Somewhere, somehow, you heard the gospel and started growing in your faith. That is the Great Commission at work. Now you, along with me and every other believer, are called to do this to this very day. We have been commissioned by Jesus Himself to help others follow Him more closely. But how? That's what this chapter will explore. I will use a series of questions to help you discover how to fulfill the Great Commission through your own life.

Who do you have an eye for?

Jesus started His ministry on this earth by selecting a group of men to follow Him closely. These men were simple men. Some were fishermen. One was a despised tax collector. One would actually become his betrayer. But the one thing they all had in common was that they were just like you and me. They were ordinary people that Jesus chose to use for an extraordinary purpose—reaching the world and raising up disciples! And it all started with an invitation to the first four disciples found in Matthew 4:18-22

18 As Jesus was walking beside the Sea of Galilee, he saw two brothers, Simon called Peter and his brother Andrew. They were casting a net into the lake, for they were fishermen. 19 "Come, follow me," Jesus said, "and I will send you out to fish for people." 20 At once they left their nets and followed him. 21 Going on from there, he saw two other brothers, James son of Zebedee and his brother John. They were in a boat with their father Zebedee, preparing their nets. Jesus called them, 22 and immediately they left the boat and their father and followed him.

I'm not sure what it was about these men that caught the eye of Jesus—but something did, and He invited them to enter His world to become something significant.

The question to you is: "who has God given you an eye for", or, "who has caught your eye and shows great spiritual potential?" Who do you see potential in and who has God given you a heart to raise up into spiritual maturity? Who is someone younger in the faith that you could see yourself investing into so they may become all that God has created them to be?

Keep in mind that anyone we lead to Christ we are responsible for discipling. We may not be the one who actually mentors them regularly. But it is our job to at least connect them to a church and expose them to other believers who will help see to it that the person you led to Christ is given every opportunity to mature spiritually. But as a starting point for now, who do you have a heart for?

Write out the name of one or two people here:

_____

What Does Your Discipleship With Them Look Like?

The next question is: what do you do practically to disciple the person God has placed on your heart? In an ideal world, this discipleship opportunity is highly relational. It's you and your mentee getting together over coffee or lunch weekly. Perhaps it is you and a couple of newer believers engaged in this journey, but I would definitely keep this to a one-on-one or at the most a one-on-three experience for all involved.

Once you determine a time and a location to meet, and the number of weeks you will do so, the next item to decide is the kind of content that you are going to walk through together. Will you walk them through this book? Is there another resource you feel might be more appropriate to address a specific need or issue your mentee is facing? Whatever you decide to do together, I encourage you to make establishing a consistent quiet time one of the chief objectives. Remember, the whole goal is to help them follow Jesus more closely. And paramount to this goal is daily Bible reading and prayer. So, establish up front what book or books of the Bible you will be reading on your own and then discussing together throughout the duration of your discipleship journey with them.

Once you establish the resource you will read together and the books of the Bible that you will both read during your daily quiet times, I highly encourage you to make a hardcore, rock solid commitment to this process. Set an appointment with your mentee weekly that you both are committed to keep—no matter what. Intentionality will be key to achieving the desired results of intimacy and spiritual growth. So, take the lead and communicate this core value to your mentee.

Which issues, specific to your mentee, need to be covered?

As I've mentioned, I am an avid believer in walking through a discipleship resource together and making sure a quiet time is established as part of the journey. However, let's face it, every person has their own set of questions and issues to be addressed. One person may really need to understand their identity in Christ. Another may really need to learn how to walk in freedom over sin. And still another may need to heal from past hurts.

What's important to understand is that while you are not their counselor, you are the conduit that God wants to use to minister to their specific, individual needs. One of my favorite titles given to Jesus is that He is the author and finisher of our faith (Hebrews 12:2). I love the imagery of Jesus with a pen in hand authoring our spiritual journey! Therefore, a few questions that would be good to cover with your mentee would be:

- What is God desiring to write into the story of your faith during this season of your life?

- What would be the name of the chapter God is currently authoring in your life?

- What is God trying to show you about Himself or about you in this season?

- What is a recurring theme that always seems to be something God is trying to hammer home in your heart as a key to your growth?

- What are some questions you would like answered about God during this season of your life?

- What do you want to learn about the most right now in regards to your faith?

- And lastly, what is God trying to teach you right now? (This is a simple but profound question when answered honestly.)

All of these questions might be good starting points for you to ask your mentee in your first couple of times together. One of the greatest exercises is exploring these answers together and then joining with the Lord to create a tailor-made plan of growth.

Special Note #1: It's important to remember that there is no way you are going to be well experienced with every topic and issue specific to your mentee. If you don't have a clue where to start when it comes to mentoring them on a particular issue specific to them, ask your pastor for some guidance. If you don't know the answer to a question they have, don't be afraid to respond with: "That's a great question. Let me do some research and get back to you." You don't have to be an expert on all issues to disciple someone. You just have to be willing to encourage them, engage in some learning yourself, and pray for them regularly. If you do these things, you will also find yourself growing exponentially as you help lead someone else to do the same!

What are the actions or attitudes in your mentee's life that could hinder their growth?

I just mentioned that Jesus is the author and finisher of our faith. Read Hebrews 12:1-2, the passage in which this title of Christ is found.

> Therefore, since we are surrounded by such a great cloud of witnesses, let us throw off everything that hinders and the sin that so easily entangles. And let us run with perseverance the race marked out for us, 2 fixing our eyes on Jesus, the pioneer and perfecter of faith. For the joy set before him he endured the cross, scorning its shame, and sat down at the right hand of the throne of God. 3 Consider him who endured such opposition from sinners, so that you will not grow weary and lose heart.

Remember, when you see the word "therefore" in the Bible, understand what it is there for! Hebrews chapter 12 follows what is known as the great hall of faith in chapter 11. The great hall of faith is a roll call of the generals of Christianity who did amazing things for God and who are now in heaven, surrounding us as great examples of those who fulfilled their purpose and persevered in their faith until the very end. In fact, a cool Bible study to do on your own or even with your mentee would be reading through the stories of everyone mentioned in Hebrews chapter 11.

But then the writer of Hebrews pivots to chapter 12 and basically says, "In light of all those who have gone before us who are now cheering us own from the sidelines of heaven, make sure you do the following things in order to follow in their footsteps." And front and center to this divine direction from heaven is "throwing off everything that hinders and the sin that so easily entangles."

"Everything that hinders" could be almost anything. But one of the things that hinders us most is the area(s) of our life where we find it hard to trust God. This could include things like our future, our finances, or key relationships within our family. I believe it is imperative to identify the "trust issues" that your mentee has with God and then encourage them, pray with them, and teach them to go to God with those things. Help them to see that God is trustworthy with all things. Unbelief is a huge hindrance and should be addressed so that it does not threaten spiritual growth.

Secondly, the writer of Hebrews states that "the sin that so easily entangles" is another huge obstacle to spiritual growth. Why? Because of the word "entangles." The sin in our life that we can't seem to shake trips us up, bogs us down, and keeps us stuck spiritually. You may need to walk through some steps to freedom such as the ones found in chapter 8 of this book. But the key principle to remember from that chapter is that our willingness to confess our sins to one another is the key to our wholeness. That means that over time, we must provide a safe environment for transparency to take place between us and our mentees. That also means that once a "sin that so easily entangles" is identified we hold our mentees accountable in a loving, yet firm and gentle way. By doing so, our mentee finds our relationship with them to be a vital key to running their race with perseverance.

Special Note #2—One particular verse that can be used to inspire your mentee is one of my favorite verses in the Bible, Hebrews 11:34,

> whose weakness was turned to strength; and who became powerful in battle and routed foreign armies.

The great men and women of faith who went before us and who are now cheering us on had many, many weaknesses. They made mistakes, wrestled through their own fears, and had to overcome the frailties of the fallen world just like you, me, and the one you are mentoring. However, through their faith, their weaknesses were turned to strengths and they were able to fight against Satan's schemes to derail their faith. That gives me great comfort and should encourage those younger in the faith as well. Our weaknesses, including the areas of our lives where we find it difficult to trust God as well as areas of sin we struggle with, can be turned to strength. And we too, along with the people we are discipling, can become strengthened to overcome anything trying to come against our faith.

Conclusion

In conclusion, let's review the basic questions to answer when it comes to establishing a nurturing, discipling relationship with someone:

1. Who has God given you an eye for? Who is one person in your life younger in their faith that you may have a heart to mentor?

2. When will you meet with them? Set a specific time, place, and number of weeks you will get together.

3. Which resource will you read together? This may be determined when you get together and discern the name of the chapter God is currently trying to author in their life.

4. Which book or books of the Bible will you read on your own and discuss whenever you get together? What is the daily prayer plan you will both establish, share with one another, and ask

each other about when you get together? (See chapter 5 in this book.)

5. Which area of life does your mentee have a harder time trusting God? Is there a sin struggle that could potentially hinder them from spiritual growth? How will these two things be addressed?

There are, of course, many other questions that could be asked to help you and your mentee get started in a discipling relationship. However, let me close by encouraging you with one verse from the Great Commission. Read Matthew 28:18-20 but look at the very last sentence:

Then Jesus came to them and said, "All authority in heaven and on earth has been given to me. Therefore, go and make disciples of all nations, baptizing them in the name of the Father and of the Son and of the Holy Spirit, and teaching them to obey everything I have commanded you. And surely I am with you always, to the very end of the age."

Jesus is with us as we set out to disciple someone else. How is He with us? Through the person of the Holy Spirit. We are to work out what the Holy Spirit is working within us personally. We are to help the ones we are discipling to do the very same. He is with us. He is in us. And He helps us to mentor others—from the inside out. So, let's close out this book with one more chapter about discipling others. This is about more than a six, eight, or twelve-week journey with someone. It's about becoming a Christian committed to doing life with others. That is the topic of our last chapter. Way to hang in there!

Spiritual Workout Week 17

*   Consider approaching someone else and inviting them to walk through this book with you. (Yes, YOU can disciple someone else!) Who would that person be that you might approach? _____)

*   Look through the five questions found in the conclusion of this chapter. What other questions do you feel is important to ask the person you desire to disciple?

- Last week, you were challenged to pick a book in the Bible to start studying next. Have you done that yet? If not, make a decision and start reading it this week!

Reflection Questions For Individual Or Small Group Use

1. What is it about the person you desire to pour into that makes you want to invest in their life?

2. What is your first step to initiate this kind of mentoring relationship with them?

3. What apprehension or fear do you have when it comes to discipling someone else?

CHAPTER 18

The Inside-Out Life

As we defined in the introduction of this book, the purest definition of a disciple is a close follower of Jesus Christ. And, according to the Great Commission found in Matthew 28:18-20, we are now called to make disciples.

It is now our honor and privilege to pass on what we have learned about Jesus to others and to intentionally mentor them into spiritual maturity through a process called discipleship. Look how the apostle Paul defined discipleship in 2 Timothy 2:2. He is speaking to Timothy, a younger brother in the Lord he mentored and is now charging to mentor others:

> "And the things you have heard me say in the
> presence of many witnesses entrust to reliable people
> who will also be qualified to teach others."

Paul is saying that Timothy should pass on to others what he has learned in order to empower others to follow Jesus closely.

But here's the deal. It would be easy for me to say, "just grab someone who seems to want to grow spiritually, put a copy of this book in their hand, and walk whoever you are mentoring through each chapter of the book." And sure, that would be a good start, along with the content of the previous chapter.

However, discipleship is far more than walking someone through a book over a couple of months. Discipleship is walking with someone through life. And who better to learn from than Jesus Himself. He is the first one to have ever discipled others—twelve of them actually.

One of my favorite disciples of Jesus was a guy named Peter. He was a fisherman and I relate to him the most out of any New Testament character. He was known to put his foot in his mouth, take radical steps of faith, fail miserably, and eventually be used by God greatly. We can learn how to disciple others by looking at how Jesus did life with Peter. The following are six things we need to do as we also do life with others.

Do life with them by declaring God's Word over them and the potential we see in them.

One key moment that Jesus had with Peter was the encounter where Jesus actually changed his name in Matthew 16:13-20. Jesus was asking people who everyone said He was. He wanted to see just how many people really grasped that He was from God. Peter answered the question correctly. "You are the Messiah, the Son of the living God." Score one for Peter! But then Jesus does something amazing. Once Peter acknowledged who Jesus was, Jesus acknowledged who Peter was going to be. He says to Peter, "And I tell you that you are Peter and upon this rock I will build my church and the gates of hell will not prevail." (v.18)

Prior to that moment, Peter's name was actually Simon, which means "small rock." Jesus is now calling him Peter, which means "large rock." Jesus saw in Peter what Peter didn't even see in himself yet. And we are to do the same with the people we are mentoring. With the help of the Holy Spirit, we need to speak life and a sense of identity over them. They need to know that we believe in them and that we affirm God's plan and purpose in their lives. They need to know that as they strive to follow Jesus closely, He is going to take them from a perception of being small in their own eyes to being great in His. And He is going to use them in such a way that not even hell can stop it!

143

Do life with them through their faith decisions.

Matthew 14:23-32 tells us about an incredible moment in the journey between Jesus and Peter. Jesus is walking on water toward the boat where the disciples were and Peter outright says, "Lord, if it is you, tell me to come to you on the water." Peter was saying, "Jesus if it's you and you can walk on water, then so can I!" You have to admire the step of faith that Peter was willing to take. He was willing to get outside of the comfortable boat and engage with Jesus in the supernatural. And boy, we all need to do the same. You need to encourage the one you are mentoring to "get outside the boat." To be willing to move beyond casual Christianity and fully contend for the faith. To not fear trusting God for the supernatural and be willing to meet with Him on those waters. And whenever God speaks to them about taking a step of faith, you need to be the one who is willing to lock arms with them, provide wise council, and even step with them outside of the boat.

Do life with them through their dilemmas.

There was a problem that ensued with the above story. Peter, in his zeal, walked on the water toward Jesus but the winds and the waves caught his attention, he lost his focus, and he sunk. And guess what, there will be times when we lose our focus and take our eyes off Jesus. And there will be times when those we are mentoring will sink as well. When they do, it is our job to help them recapture their focus by pointing them back to Christ. We need to remind them of Philippians 1:6, which says that He who began a good work in them will carry it on to completion. There may be surprises along the way, unexpected twists and turns, and even downturns they might experience. But in the midst of those challenging times we need to remind them to turn their eyes toward the Lord—their source of help. Be the hands of Jesus to the one you are discipling and when they sink, help them regain their footing.

Do life with them by helping them develop their inner delight.

Ok, this is one of my favorite chapters in the Peter and Jesus journey. The time had come for Jesus to reveal to His disciples that He would be crucified. Peter couldn't believe it and actually began to rebuke Jesus. Jesus turned to Peter and said in Matthew 16:23, "Get behind me

Satan. You don't have in mind the things of God, but the things of man." I would say this story escalated quickly! But what was really happening in that moment was that Peter fell prey to a worldly mindset. He certainly didn't have an eternal perspective and was immature in His understanding concerning the full nature of why Jesus was on the earth in the first place. And Jesus equated this type of thinking with Satan himself, whose goal it is to cause people to be so caught up in this world that they never acknowledge the world to come. The devil's goal is to blind them to the truth of Jesus' mission to save them from this temporary life and grant them eternal life in the world to come. It is this kind of carnal thinking that is absolutely contrary to a Christ filled life.

Our job in mentoring someone in the faith is bound to include some difficult conversations along the way. We will need to lovingly confront them, or as it has been said, "care-front" them for worldliness that is not yet under the authority of Jesus. And the questions we need to pose to them include: "What are you setting your affections on? What holds your heart strings? Is Jesus really your first love in every area of your life?" These questions reveal where a person's true inner delight is and whether or not they are setting their hearts on the things above or the things below (Colossians 3:1). It is our job to remind those we mentor that being a true disciple means denying ourselves, suffering for the cause of Christ, and choosing to find life and inner delight in following Him closely.

Do life with them through their denial.

But what happens when the person you are discipling does fail miserably? What if they back slide? What if they disappear for a few weeks and don't show up for church or your one on one meetings? And what if they start to drift away from their commitment to discipleship? Peter did this. He failed miserably at one of the most important crossroads of Jesus' whole ministry—the point of His crucifixion. He basically denied Jesus to a junior high girl at a campfire. Oh man, talk about a point of spineless failure.

Peter forgot about Jesus, but Jesus did not forget about him after He died and rose again. In fact, there is a moment where Jesus specifically tells the others to go find Peter. He reinstates him in such a way that it reaffirms the identity of Peter as the large rock we spoke about at the start of this chapter.

Jesus did not give up on Peter and we do not need to give up on people either. In chapter six I mentioned being a part of a church that chases people down. We need to take a long-haul approach to discipling people and refuse to give up on them—especially when they demonstrate brokenness and contrition the way Peter did.

Do life with them through their dreams.

And last but not least, we need to do life with people and celebrate with them when their dreams come true. In fact, one of the most spiritual things we can do is celebrate with those we are mentoring. We need to be their biggest fans, their biggest cheerleaders, and the one who will affirm them for their accomplishments. In fact, if you want to gain continued influence with the people you lead, be an encourager and one who will celebrate with others. I believe this quality was central to the personality of Jesus. And so, can you imagine the smile that must have been on Jesus' face after He returned to heaven and witnessed Peter preach the gospel to 3000 people? What a dream come true, for Peter and for Jesus! The one you are mentoring may never preach to the multitudes, but they will hit spiritual milestones and will need to hear your voice of celebration over them.

Conclusion

My dream is to see a movement again in the body of Christ where we are intentionally making disciples—close followers of Jesus. To do so means we have to be willing to do life with people. We need to see in them what they do not see in themselves and be willing to walk with them through thick and thin until they are ready to disciple someone else. That's the multiplying effect of discipleship and that is how the church will fulfill the Great Commission.

Spiritual Workout Week 18

- Plan the next leg in your own spiritual journey in regards to your time with God. Answer these questions:

- One last time.....What will you read next in your Bible?
  _____

- What will you pray for each day of the week moving forward?
  Monday_____
  Tuesday_____
  Wednesday_____
  Thursday_____
  Friday_____

- Will you continue with the IRA Bible study method or try something different? _____

- Who is one lost, unchurched person, you are committed to reach from this point forward? _____

- Again, who is the one person in your life that you would like to mentor? _____

Reflection Questions For Individual Or Small Group Use

1. Which of the above dynamics from Peter's life can you most relate to? (His foot in mouth syndrome? His willingness to take radical steps of faith? His failure at times and short-sighted thinking? His need for a second chance? His untapped potential that was finally lived out?)

2. In the last chapter, you identified one person you may be interested in mentoring. What dynamics of Peter's story can you see in that person?

3. As this book and resource come to an end, which of the four CORE commitments will be the easiest for you to continue with? The most challenging? (Connect with God, Offer Him Everything, Release Your Ministry, Engage in Outreach).

Conclusion

One more time, look at Colossians 2:6-7,

> "So then, just as you received Christ Jesus as Lord, continue to live your lives in him, rooted and built up in him, strengthened in the faith as you were taught, and overflowing with thankfulness."

We are simply called to continue ...to continue to work out the CORE of our salvation:

We Must Continue To Connect with God.

We must continue to pray. As the days unfold before us, it will be His presence that anchors our soul during the storms of life. We must continue to become people of the Word. The Word safeguards us, protects us, and equips us to live a life on the offense in the kingdom of God— advancing His purposes against the kingdom of darkness. And we must continue to attend church and build Christian community in our lives. It is through the local church and the relationships we form with the body of Christ that our lives are enriched the most. We must continue to chase people down!

We Must Continue To Offer God Our Everything.

Remember, we express our love for God through our obedience. Jesus didn't die on the cross to be a part of our life, He died to become our life (Colossians 3:4). Our highest form of worship isn't offering God our song on Sunday mornings, but offering Him our lives throughout the week as a living sacrifice. We must continue to offer God our everything, because our God offered everything for us through His son Jesus Christ. This is perhaps the greatest key to finding joy in the journey between now and heaven.

We Must Continue To Release Our Ministry.

We must continue to steward our time, talents, and our treasure for the glory of God. We must continue to allow God to shape purpose from our past and we must continue to discern the works He prepared in advance for us to do (Ephesians 2:10). We must not allow fear to keep us from stepping out in faith and we must continue to be humbled by the very thought that God has chosen to use us. We must continue to release our ministry.

We Must Continue To Engage In Outreach & Missions.

Although we do not know the time or the hour that Christ will return, look at one more sign that will indicate that our blessed hope is near from Matthew 24:14, "And this gospel of the kingdom will be preached in the whole world as a testimony to all nations, and then the end will come." One thing that will take place before Christ returns is the proclamation of the gospel to the four corners of the world. And get this, our participation in the Great Commission can actually expedite the return of Christ! Therefore, we must continue to engage people with the gospel. This starts with our closest friends, family, co-workers, and neighbors and extends to the nations. We must continue to give. We must continue to go. We must continue to engage in personal outreach and world missions. And we must disciple people, through the power of the Holy Spirit, into deeper levels of spiritual maturity.

CORE Evaluation

When you sign up for a gym membership, you are usually offered a free consultation to evaluate your starting point. They weigh you, take your blood pressure, measure your body mass index, and even take your picture to give you a true before picture as you start your journey toward health. That is what this short evaluation is all about-discovering your spiritual baseline as you start this discipleship playbook. Your leader will walk through this guide with you in your next meeting.

C-Connect with God

What are you currently doing for your time with the Lord each day? What are some specific prayer requests that you have in this season of your life?

_____

_____

_____

_____

What do you feel is your biggest hindrance to spending time with God each day? What helps you the most to stay on track spiritually?

_____

_____

_____

_____

Describe a season in your life when you were closest to the Lord. What made that season so significant? What were you doing in that season to draw close to the Lord?

_____

_____

_____

_____

O-Offer God Your Everything
Briefly write out your definition of surrender:

_____

_____

_____

_____

Is there any area of your life that you have not fully surrendered to God?
Yes   No

Which area of life do you have the most difficulty surrendering to the Lord?

R-Release Your Ministry
Do you feel like you have a clear understanding of what your spiritual and ministry gifts are?

Yes   No   Somewhat

If so, what are they?

_____

_____

_____

_____

Are you currently using these gifts to the glory of God?

Yes   No   Sometimes

If so, how?

_____

_____

_____

_____

E-Engage In Personal Outreach & Missions

Do you feel comfortable sharing your faith with the unchurched people in your life? Yes   No

Have you ever been trained to do so? Yes   No

If you could take a foreign missions trip to anywhere in the world, where would you go and why?

_____

_____

_____

_____

APPENDIX 2

Developing your personal testimony

Your personal testimony is your own eyewitness account of what Jesus Christ has done in your life. It is important to realize that no one can talk you out of your testimony because it is just that—your story and your firsthand personal knowledge of what God has done for you. Your testimony is simply your evidence of a God who is real and has transformed your life. It's yours. Don't allow the devil, your friends, or even your own flesh tell you otherwise.

This brief yet powerful exercise has powerful implications for your faith. Romans 12:11 states, "They triumphed over him (Satan) by the blood of the Lamb and by the word of their testimony; they did not love their lives so much as to shrink from death."

There are three keys to our victory as believers in this verse—the blood of Christ, our testimony, and a sold-out commitment to love God with all of our hearts. Our testimony, central to this victory, is the expression of our faith concerning what God has already done (the blood of the Lamb) and what we are committed to do from this point forward (love Him to the point of refusing to even shrink back from death should we be persecuted). Your testimony looks back on what God has done and who you look to become now that your life is in Christ. It is the story of your salvation but also the story of the current work God is doing in your life now.

Our salvation testimony is usually comprised of three parts—*before, how, and after.* The *before* is all about who we were prior to our salvation experience. The *how* is just that—how we came to Christ. Did a friend lead you to Christ? Did you give your heart to the Lord at church? How. And lastly, the *after* is all about what God has done in your life since becoming a Christian and what He is currently doing in your heart now.

Take a moment and write out a paragraph for each of these three components. As you do, allow the Holy Spirit to connect the dots for you and help you to realize once again the work God has done, and is doing, in your life. And then make a commitment to share this story with others!

Before

_____

_____

_____

_____

How

_____

_____

_____

_____

After

_____

_____

_____

_____

Zero Based Budget

Budget

Note: The goal of this exercise is a "zero based budget." In other words, when you finish your budget, there should not be any money that isn't assigned a category within this budget.

Income Categories (Monthly)

Your income $_____

Spouse income $_____

Other $_____

Total monthly income $_____

Giving

Tithing $_____- (10% of your take home pay. Some people choose to tithe off of their gross)

Other $_____

Other $_____

Total monthly giving: $_____

Savings

Monthly Retirement $_____ (if not already taken out of your check)

Monthly cash savings $_____

Total monthly savings: $_____

Expense Categories

Housing

Mortgage/Rent $_____

Power Bill $_____

Cable $_____

Water $_____

Netflix $_____

Trash $_____

Yard $_____

Other $_____

Other $_____

Other $_____

Other $_____

Total monthly housing: $_____

Vehicle

Payment #1 $_____

Payment #2 $_____

Car insurance $_____

Total fuel $_____

Repairs $_____

Tags $_____ (add up approximate amount and divide by 12)

*Total monthly vehicle: $*_____

Food
Monthly groceries $_____

Monthly eating out budget $_____

*Total monthly food: $*_____

Medical
Doctor's appointments/co-pays $_____
(**based on last year's totals, come up with an approximate amount that you should set aside monthly for doctor visits for your family)

Life insurance $_____

Dental expenses $_____

Eye doctor expenses $_____

Total monthly medication expense $_____

*Total monthly medical: $*_____

Children
Daycare $_____

Kid activity #1 $_____ (sports, hobby, etc)

Kid activity #2 $_____

Kid activity #3 $_____

Kid activity #4 $_____

Tuition/dues $_____ (add up approximate amount and divide by 12)

Total monthly allowance for all kids $_____

Total monthly children expenses: $_____

Debt pay down expenses (other than car and mortgage)
Debt #1 _____$_____

Debt #2 _____ $_____

Debt #3 _____ $_____

Debt #4 _____ $_____

Debt #5 _____ $_____

Total monthly debt expenses: $_____

Other

Cell Phone $_____

Haircuts $_____

Clothing $_____

Monthly subscription #1: _____ $_____

Monthly subscription #2: _____ $_____

Monthly subscription #3: _____ $_____

Yearly subscription #1: _____ $_____

Yearly subscription #2: _____ $_____

Yearly subscription #3: _____ $_____

Other: _____ $_____

Other: _____ $_____

Total other expenses: $_____

Total Expenses

Total monthly giving: $_____

Total monthly savings: $_____

Total monthly housing: $_____

Total monthly vehicle: $_____

Total monthly food: $_____

Total monthly medical: $_____

Total monthly children expenses: $_____

Total monthly debt expenses: $_____

Total other expenses: $_____

Grand Total Expenses: $_____

Grand Totals:

Total Monthly Income $_____

Grand Total Expenses: $_____

Surplus/Difference: $_____

DISC Personality Profile:

This is a simple starting point to the DISC personality profile. Very simple in fact but actually pretty revealing. Score yourself from 1-5 (1=never, 5=always) for each statement under the four different blocks. Add up your scores for each block and place the number in the (Total_____) line.

Sample: I have responded to each statement by boldening my score for each statement.

simple Discovery–My personality / Leadership Style _____					
TOTAL **23**	Never	Rarely	Sometimes	Often	Always
I am assertive, demanding, & decisive.	1	2	3	**4**	5
I enjoy doing multiple tasks at once.	1	2	3	4	**5**
I thrive in a challenge -based environment.	1	2	3	4	**5**
I think about tasks above others or myself.	1	2	3	**4**	**5**
I am motivated by accomplishment & authority	1	2	3	4	**5**

Now, take the test following the above format. After you finish, I'll explain how to interpret the results!

simple Discovery—My personality / Leadership
Style _____

TOTAL _____	Never	Rarely	Sometimes	Often	Always
I am assertive, demanding, & decisive.	1	2	3	4	5
I enjoy doing multiple tasks at once.	1	2	3	4	5
I thrive in a challenge -based environment.	1	2	3	4	5
I think about tasks above others or myself.	1	2	3	4	5
I am motivated by accomplishment & authority	1	2	3	4	5

TOTAL _____	Never	Rarely	Sometimes	Often	Always
I enjoy influencing and inspiring people	1	2	3	4	5
I am optimistic about others.	1	2	3	4	5
I tend to be the life of the party.	1	2	3	4	5
I think about motivating people.	1	2	3	4	5
I am motivated by recognition and approval.	1	2	3	4	5

TOTAL _____	Never	Rarely	Sometimes	Often	Always
I thrive in consistent environments over changing ones	1	2	3	4	5
I prefer specifics over generalizations..	1	2	3	4	5
I enjoy small groups of people.	1	2	3	4	5
I prefer being a member of a team over. leading them.	1	2	3	4	5
I am motivated by stability & support..	1	2	3	4	5

TOTAL _____	Never	Rarely	Sometimes	Often	Always
I typically do not take big risks.	1	2	3	4	5
I love tasks, order & details..	1	2	3	4	5
I am right most of the time.	1	2	3	4	5
I comply with clearly defined rules.	1	2	3	4	5
I am motivated by quality & correctness..	1	2	3	4	5

Interpreting the results

Understanding your score and personality is easy. Block #1 is your score for the "D" trait, Block #2 is your "I" score, Block #3 is your "S" score, and Block #4 is your "C" score. In the above example I scored 23 for the "D" trait. Now you can read the descriptions for each personality and the corresponding "opportunities for personal growth."

DISCOVERING YOUR PERSONALITY–OPPORTUNITIES FOR PERSONAL GROWTH

If you are a "D" – Dominant, Direct, Task oriented, Decisive, Organized, Outgoing, Outspoken

A. Strive to listen to other people more attentively.

B. Try to be less controlling and domineering.

C. Develop a greater appreciation for the opinions, feelings and desires of others.

D. Put more energy into personal relationships.

E. Show your support for the other team members.

If you are an "I" – Influential, Interested in people, Witty, Easygoing, Outgoing, People Oriented

A. Weigh the pros and cons before making a decision; be less impulsive.

B. Remember to help with tasks more.

C. Exercise control over your actions, words and emotions.

D. Focus more on details and facts.

E. Talk less; listen more.

If you are a "S" – Steady, Stability, Analytical, People oriented, Introverted

A. Consider how change is healthy. Try to change more willingly.

B Be more direct in your interactions.

C. Focus on overall goals of your family or group rather than specific procedures.

D. Deal with confrontation constructively.

E. Develop more flexibility.

F. Try to show more initiative.

If you are a "C" – Compliant, Competent, Task oriented, Goal oriented, Introverted

A. Concentrate on doing the right things – not just doing things right.

B. Be less critical of others' ideas and methods.

C. Respond more quickly to accomplish others' goals.

D. Strive to build relationships with other people and family members.

E. Be more decisive.

F. Focus less on facts and more on people.

APPENDIX 5

Spiritual Gifts Test

1. Read each statement and give yourself a score from 1–5. 1=Almost never, 5=Almost Always. Record your score for each statement on the following page. Note: Don't overthink this. Just write down the first score that comes to mind and move on to the next one!

2. After you record your scores, you will then add the scores from left to right and record your total. This total is your score for the spiritual gift listed to the right.

3. Your highest scores reveal your top spiritual gifts.

4. Read through the spiritual gifts descriptions for further understanding. I encourage you to talk through your results with your pastor, small group, or accountability partner.

*Should you have any confusion with this test, there is a brief video explanation available on the book's website.

SPIRITUAL GIFTS QUESTIONS

1. I like organizing services and events.

2. I enjoy starting new churches.

3. I enjoy working with my hands.

4. I can tell when someone is insincere.

5. I pray for the lost daily.

6. Encouraging others is a high priority in my life.

7. Believing God for our daily needs is important to me.

8. Influencing others for the kingdom of God through finances is extremely important to me.

9. I look for opportunities to pray for the sick.

10. I enjoy doing the little things that others do not.

11. I enjoy having people come to my home.

12. I enjoy spending hours in prayer for other people.

13. Education is very important to me.

14. I tend to motivate others to get involved.

15. My heart hurts when I see other hurting.

16. I believe God will use me to enact His miracles.

17. I enjoy sharing the gospel with other people groups and nationalities.

18. I've devoted considerable time to mastering my voice and/or instrument.

19. Caring for the hurting is paramount in my eyes.

20. The willful sin of others really aggravates me.

21. I enjoy serving behind the scenes.

22. I enjoy creating outlines of the Bible.

23. God has used me to interpret a heavenly language.

24. I enjoy the book of Proverbs more than any other book in the Bible.

25. I am passionate about managing details.

26. I prefer to pioneer new ministry projects.

27. I consider myself a craftsman or craftswoman.

28. I sense when situations are spiritually unhealthy.

29. I am greatly concerned about seeing the lost saved.

30. I try to come across as loving and caring.

31. Asking God for a list of big things is exciting to me.

32. I find ways to give offerings above my tithes.

33. I believe miraculous healing is for this day and age.

34. Helping others is one of my highest achievements.

35. Creating a warm & welcoming home is important to me.

36. I am burdened to pray for situations in the world.

37. People seek me out to learn more about the kingdom of God.

38. I prefer to take the lead whenever necessary.

39. I'm very sensitive to sad stories.

40. Miracles often happen when I'm nearby.

41. Living in another country to benefit the gospel is exciting to me.

42. I desire to serve the church through worship.

43. I enjoy connecting, caring, and coaching others.

44. Confronting someone with sin in their life is not hard.

45. It bothers me when people sit around and do nothing.

46. I share Biblical truth with others in hopes of their personal growth.

47. I pray in tongues daily.

48. When I study scripture God gives me unique insights.

49. Creating a task list is easy and enjoyable for me.

50. I am attracted to ministries that start new churches.

51. Building something with my hands is very rewarding to me.

52. I can pinpoint issues or problems before others.

53. I enjoy sharing the gospel with a total stranger.

54. I look for ways to be an encouragement to other people.

55. I trust that God has my back in every situation.

56. Making more money means I can give more.

57. God has used me to bring healing to those who are sick.

58. Being a part of the process is fulfilling to me.

59. I tend to make total strangers feel at home.

60. People often describe me as a prayer warrior.

61. I enjoy knowing biblical details and helping others to understand.

62. I delegate responsibilities to accomplish tasks.

63. I am motivated to help those who are less fortunate.

64. I have a constant hunger to see God's miraculous power.

65. I focus a lot on reaching the world for Christ.

66. I gain my deepest satisfaction through leading others in vocal or instrumental worship.

67. I enjoy walking with someone in times of direst.

68. I enjoy hearing passionate and clear preaching of the truth.

69. I like to do small things that others pass over.

70. I prefer to teach the Bible topically rather than verse by verse.

71. Praying in the Spirit is encouraging and important to me.

72. When faced with difficulty I tend to make wise decisions and choices.

SPIRITUAL GIFTS RATINGS

1. Almost Never	2. Seldom	3. Sometimes	4. Frequently	5. Almost Always
			Total	Gifts
1. _____	25. _____	49. _____	_____	A. Administration
2. _____	26. _____	50. _____	_____	B. Apostleship
3. _____	27. _____	51. _____	_____	C. Craftsmanship
4. _____	28. _____	52. _____	_____	D. Discernment
5. _____	29. _____	53. _____	_____	E. Evangelism
6. _____	30. _____	54. _____	_____	F. Exhortation
7. _____	31. _____	55. _____	_____	G. Faith
8. _____	32. _____	56. _____	_____	H. Giving
9. _____	33. _____	57. _____	_____	I. Healing
10. _____	34. _____	58. _____	_____	J. Helps
11. _____	35. _____	59. _____	_____	K. Hospitality
12. _____	36. _____	60. _____	_____	L. Intercession
13. _____	37. _____	61. _____	_____	M. Knowledge
14. _____	38. _____	62. _____	_____	N. Leadership
15. _____	39. _____	63. _____	_____	O. Mercy
16. _____	40. _____	64. _____	_____	P. Miracles
17. _____	41. _____	65. _____	_____	Q. Missionary

1. Almost Never	2. Seldom	3. Sometimes	4. Frequently	5. Almost Always
18. _____	42. _____	66. _____	_____	R. Music / Worship
19. _____	43. _____	67. _____	_____	S. Pastor / Shepherd
20. _____	44. _____	68. _____	_____	T. Prophecy
21. _____	45. _____	69. _____	_____	U. Service
22. _____	46. _____	70. _____	_____	V. Teaching
23. _____	47. _____	71. _____	_____	W. Tongues (And Interpre tations)
24. _____	48. _____	72. _____	_____	X. Wisdon

GIFT DEFINITIONS AND SCRIPTURE REFERENCES

The following contains definitions of the Spiritual gifts. While not meant to be dogmatic or final, these definitions and supporting scriptures do correspond to characteristics of the gifts as expressed in the Gift Questionnaire.

A. ADMINISTRATION

The gift of administration is the divine strength or ability to organize multiple tasks and groups of people to accomplish these tasks. (Luke 14:28-30, Acts 6:1-7, 1 Corinthians 12:28)

B. APOSTLESHIP

The gift of apostleship is the divine strength or ability to pioneer new churches and ministries through planting, overseeing, and training. (Acts 15:22-35, 1 Corinthians 12:28, 2 Corinthians 12:12, Galatians 2:7-10, Ephesians 4:11-14)

C. CRAFTSMANSHIP

The gift of craftsmanship is the divine strength or ability to plan, build, and work with your hands in construction environments to accomplish multiple ministry applications. (Exodus 30:22, 31:3-11, 2 Chronicles 34:9-13, Acts 18:2-3)

D. DISCERNMENT

The gift of discernment is the divine strength or ability to spiritually identify falsehood and to distinguish between right and wrong motives and situations. (Matthew 6:21-23, Acts 5:1-11, 16:16-18, 1 Corinthians 12:10, 1 John 4:1-6)

E. EVANGELISM

The gift of evangelism is the divine strength or ability to help non-Christians take the necessary steps to becoming a born-again Christian. (Acts 8:5-6, Acts 8:26-40, Acts 14:21, Acts 21:8, Ephesians 4:11-14)

F. EXHORTATION

The gift of exhortation is the divine strength or ability to encourage others through the written or spoken word and Biblical truth. (Acts. 14:22, Romans 12:8, 1 Timothy 4:31, Hebrews 10:24-25)

G. FAITH

The gift of faith is the divine strength or ability to believe in God for unseen supernatural results in every arena of life. (Acts 11:22-24, Romans 4:18-21, 1 Corinthians 12:9, Hebrews 11)

H. GIVING

The gift of giving is the divine strength or ability to produce wealth and to give by tithes and offerings for the purpose of advancing the Kingdom of God on earth.

(Mark 12:41-44, Romans 12:8, 2 Corinthians 8:1-7, 9:2-7)

I. HEALING

The gift of healing is the divine strength or ability to act as an intermediary in faith, prayer, and by the laying on of hands for the healing of physical and mental illnesses. (Acts 3:1-10, Acts 9:32-35, Acts 28:7-10, 1 Corinthians 12:9, 28)

J. HELPS

The gift of helps is the divine strength or ability to work in a supportive role for the accomplishment of tasks in Christian ministry. (Mark 15:40-41, Acts 9:36, Romans 16:1-2, 1 Corinthians 12:28)

K. HOSPITALITY

The gift of hospitality is the divine strength or ability to create warm, welcoming environments for others in places such as your home, office or church. (Acts 16:14-15, Romans 12:13, Romans 16:23, Hebrews 13:1-2, 1 Peter 4:9)

L. INTERCESSION

The gift of intercession is the divine strength or ability to stand in the gap in prayer for someone, something, or someplace believing for profound results. (Hebrews 7:25, Colossians 1:9-12, Colossians 4:12-13, James 5:14-15)

M. KNOWLEDGE

The gift of knowledge is the divine strength or ability to bring clarity and to understand situations and circumstances often accompanied by a word from God. (Acts 5:1-11, 1 Corinthians 12:8, Colossians 2:2-3)

N. LEADERSHIP

The gift of leadership is the divine strength or ability to influence people at their level while directing and focusing them on the big picture, vision or idea. (Romans 12:8, 1 Timothy 3:1-13, 1 Timothy 5:17, Hebrews 13:17)

O. MERCY

The gift of mercy is the divine strength or ability to feel empathy and to care for those who are hurting in any way. (Matthew 9:35-36, Mark 9:41, Romans 12:8, 1 Thessalonians 5:14)

P. MIRACLES

The gift of miracles is the divine strength or ability to alter the natural outcomes of life in a supernatural way through prayer, faith and divine direction. (Acts 9:36-42, 19:11-12, 20:7-12, Romans 15:18-19, 1 Corinthians 12:10, 28)

Q. MISSIONARY

The gift of missions is the divine strength or ability to reach others outside of your culture and nationality; while in most cases living in that culture or nation. (Acts 8:4, Acts 13:2-3, Acts 22:21, Romans 10:15)

R. MUSIC / WORSHIP

The gift of music / worship is the divine strength or ability to sing, dance, or play an instrument primarily for the purpose of helping others worship God.

(Deuteronomy 31:22, 1 Samuel 16:16, 1 Chronicles 16:41-42, 2 Chronicles 5:12-13, 34:12, Psalm 150)

S. PASTOR / SHEPHERD

The gift of pastor / shepherd is the divine strength or ability to care for the personal needs of others by nurturing and mending life issues. (John 10:1-18, Ephesians 4:11-14, 1 Timothy 3:1-7, 1 Peter 5:1-3)

T. PROPHECY

The gift of prophecy is the divine strength or ability to boldly speak and bring clarity to scriptural and doctrinal truth, in some cases foretelling God's plan (Acts. 2:37-40, Acts 7:51-53, Acts 26:24-29, 1 Corinthians 14:1-4, 1 Thessalonians 1:5)

U. SERVICE

The gift of serving is the divine strength or ability to do small or great tasks in working for the overall good of the body of Christ. (Acts 6:1-7, Romans 12:7, Galatians 6:10, 2 Timothy 1:16-18, Titus 3:14)

V. TEACHING

The gift of teaching is the divine strength or ability to study and learn from the Scriptures primarily to bring understanding and depth to other Christians. (Acts 18:24-28, Acts 20:20-21, 1 Corinthians 12:28, Ephesians 4:11-14)

W. TONGUES (and interpretations)

The gift of tongues is the divine strength or ability to pray in a heavenly language to encourage your spirit and to commune with God. The gift of tongues is often accompanied by interpretation and should be used appropriately. (Acts 2:1-13, 1 Corinthians 12:10, 14:1-14)

X. WISDOM

The gift of wisdom is the divine strength or ability to apply the truths of Scripture in a practical way, producing the fruitful outcome and character of Jesus Christ.

(Acts 6:3, 10, 1 Corinthians 2:6-13, 1 Corinthians 12:8)